HOW TO MAKE A FORTUNE IN FINDERS' FEES

ALSO BY JACK PAYNE

THE ENCYCLOPEDIA OF LITTLE-KNOWN, HIGHLY PROFITABLE BUSINESS OPPORTUNITIES
(1971, Frederick Fell Publishers, Inc., New York)

HOW TO MAKE A FORTUNE IN FINDERS' FEES

by

Jack Payne

Frederick Fell Publishers, Inc. New York

EDITOR'S NOTE: While the information published in this book is believed to be from reliable sources, the publishers cannot guarantee them. No warranty or representation of any kind is made as to the accuracy of these data; all opportunities reported are subject to errors, omissions, obsolescence, or withdrawal without notice. This book was compiled and written for news value and public information only. Therefore, the publishers accept no responsibility for contacts, negotiations, or business agreements that might result from publishing this type information.

Also, because all submitted material contained has been *rewritten* by the author, none of it should be considered as a *direct* offering on the part of the source given—only as an invitation to write for further details.

It is recommended that the course of prudence and thorough investigation be exercised by every reader, independently, in dealings with all parties, prior to the consummation of business transactions of any kind.

For information address:
Frederick Fell Publishers, Inc.
386 Park Avenue South
New York, N.Y. 10016

Library of Congress Catalog Card No. 73-80450

Published simultaneously in Canada by
George J. McLeod, Limited, Toronto 2B, Ontario

Manufactured in the United States of America

International Standard Book No. 0-8119-0225-0

To Jeff

Prolog / Acknowledgments

LIKE MOST HUMAN BEINGS, we hid our many mistakes in the closet in our earlier, frustrating years of trying to make money in the Finders' fee business. So did many others.

We *eventually* obtained our "Trial and Error" *experience* degree from that sacrosanct old institution, The College of Hard Knocks. So did many others.

It was only in the 1950s that we engaged extensively, personally, in the Finders' fee business, and, after countless heartbreaking blunders, learned to the point where we found it most rewarding. Since switching to full-time publishing of all kinds of business opportunities, *including specific Finders' fee opportunities,* and carefully observing the failures and successes of many other Finders since, we feel we are now able to "put it all together." This we have attempted to do in this book.

We want to thank all the wonderful hard-working Finders whose experiences we're relating in this book, as well as our own.

Overall objective: We want *you* to graduate from this "school" too. We want *you* to graduate *without* having to go through the same tedious, laborious, "trial and error" methods of learning that we all employed. In this book we've tried to give you a practical "short course" in this, *perhaps the most lucrative of all fields of business.*

Once mastered, we think you'll find this field fast, exciting, even downright hypnotizing . . . as we, and many others, have.

You will, therefore, find this a go-go, "uptick" book—*all the way.*

Jack Payne

Contents

HOW TO MAKE A FORTUNE IN FINDERS' FEES

CHAPTER 1

Finders' Fees—Enormous Earnings Potential

IN 1966, A MISSOURI MAN earned $90,000 on a *single* business transaction. What transaction? The sale of a huge tonnage of long-grain rice. In 1969, a Floridian made $65,000 on a *single* sale of a European antique collection. Again, his "pay-off" was a Finder's fee. In 1968, a Texas man collected a *single* fee of $115,000 on the sale of a ranch . . . A New Yorker, in 1967, pocketed some $400,000 cash, plus stock, as the result of a merger of two manufacturing companies . . . A California subscriber made $38,000 by finding a buyer for jade from Taiwan in 1971 . . . From 1963 to 1970, an Indiana man earned a steady *yearly* income averaging $15,000—*extra* pocket money—by finding sellers of rare coin collections for three different multimillionaire buyers. Yes, *all* of this money, taken in by *each* of these individuals, was in "Finders'" fees.

Where *are* "Finders'" fee opportunities?

Walk through a shopping center, a discount store. Drive through any industrial complex, visit any dock where the cargo is being unloaded by longshoreman. Watch any office building or high-rise business structure of any type, either as it's going up, or the hub-bub of activity through its windows after it's occupied and functioning. Attend an auction. Read the classified sections of newspapers. Read the ads and contents of trade and business magazines in many fields. Chances are great that a *Finder*—somewhere along the line—had much to do with the creation of the business momentum that you will have observed. This is the beauty of this business: Like a broad spectrum antibiotic, attacking the zillions of bacteria in your own body's blood stream and devouring them, the "Finder" reaches into every remote area of American business . . . and collects his fees. *His horizons are as broad as the composite whole of our American economy itself.*

Here are just a few examples of Finders' fee offerings taken from recent issues of *BUSINESS OPPORTUNITIES DIGEST:* Fees for finding insurance policy holders willing to convert their insurance premiums into tax-deductible items . . . For uncovering hidden estates . . . For finding bulk buyers for a new bio-degradable cleaner selling at an amazing 65% off . . . For finding buyers, sellers and traders in blocked, frozen or restricted foreign currencies . . . For finding those willing to *rent* letters of credit . . . 5% fees for *renting* your own collateral, *and having it too* . . . "Package Travel Tours"—set up trips abroad, get *free* hotel rooms for yourself, earn good commissions, *and Finders' fees* . . . 5% fees for finding big quantities of cosmetic and pharmaceutical products available for resale . . . Find sellers or buyers for *any kind* of production tools or equipment and earn a 5% fee for each "closed" deal . . . Find those willing to join an exclusive Mexican Land Syndicate and earn 3% fees . . . Earn fees of $1.00 per bushel on the sale of Triticale grain . . . 5% fees for selling elephants . . . 5,000 green stamps for locating financing.

Rare? Unusual? Odd? Yes. But, we have presented this small handful of way-out examples merely to show you the long-tentacled "reach" of this Finders' fee business.

Opinion: You, too, *can* earn fabulous money in the "Finding" business—*if* you set it up "right," work at it "right," and cash-in on it "right." The purpose of this book is to show you the way. Our credentials? In addition to our own experiences, since 1963, examining just about every kind of Finders' fee offering imaginable, coming across our editorial desk at *BUSINESS OPPORTUNITIES DIGEST, just about every single day.*

In the ensuing chapters we will lay out a road map for you to follow. We will tell you about the most lucrative fields, how to set up your own Finding service, the equipment and supplies you'll need, the know-how and where-how you'll need.

We sincerely hope this book will lead you to eventually becoming the self-made millionaire you'd long hoped for . . . but never really counted on.

CHAPTER 2

What Are Finders' Fees? How Do You Start?

WHEN YOU WERE A CHILD your mother probably told you to *find* that expensive stuffed tiger she'd bought you for Christmas. Maybe you were asked to *find* a jack-knife on a treasure hunt; perhaps *find* a new girl friend for your lonely sister, Suzie.

A few descriptions of the word "find" from a dictionary tell us that it means "to get by searching," "to reach; attain." This is *precisely* what this book is all about. This is *precisely* what we are trying to enable you to do through it—not find lost marbles or lollypops—but now that you are an adult "to get by searching, to reach, to attain"—*in order to build a small fortune for yourself.*

In business life, too, the meaning of the word "find" is just that. Where a sale of something is involved, you find a *buyer*. Where an acquisition of something is involved, you find a *seller*.

We've found that the very best way to find one party to a business transaction is to look in your own local community (buyer or seller), then match up his needs with those of another party (buyer or seller) in any part of the world *away* from your own local community. However, there is also no reason why you can't be instrumental in bringing together two parties—one in California, the other in New York—either, even if you live in

Alaska. Many do. Many make *fortunes* doing it—moreover—and both ways.

HOW TO BE AN EFFECTIVE FINDER

The requisite importance of being esoteric, controlling all initial information, shrouding it in secrecy, hugging it to your breast like a Mother Hen, cannot be emphasized too strongly. This, *until* you have something in writing from at least one of the two parties to a potential business deal, something "standupable" in a court of law, something that will *legally* protect your fee, if and when, of course, the deal is ultimately finalized as a result of your initial "bringing together" act! In Chapter 4, under the sub-title, THIS MATTER OF PROTECTING YOURSELF—THROUGH EXCHANGES OF LETTERS, AGREEMENTS AND CONTRACTS, we'll tell you all about the "how" of this.

Those of you old enough to remember the post World War II "5 Percenter" can analagize him, to an extent, to the current-day Finder. In the late 1940s it was not uncommon for a 5 Percenter to take big newspaper ads stating he had big quantities of something that was in short supply. (In reality he had nothing.) Then, upon indications of interest, he'd start looking, scratching, frantically searching. In these post-war days of abundance, this extreme exercise is usually not necessary. But . . . the old economic equation of supply and demand *always* creates a situation where somebody needs something, urgently, quickly, and can't come up with the right source in time. This is where *you,* as a professional Finder, come in. If your contacts are widespread, reliable, highly sales and profit oriented, basically sound Businessmen, and *many in number,* you have a chance of filling the void and coming out with a pocket stuffed with green—*time and again.*

THE STARTING POINT—IMPRESSION GETS YOU GOING

If you know of a buyer of opals in the United States, and you know of a seller of opals in Australia, you naturally contact each, probably by letter. If you write letters to each, scrawled in hand, on lined tablet paper (you'd be surprised how many of these we receive in ad form at *BUSINESS OPPORTUNITIES DIGEST*), forget it. Neither party will have any confidence in you whatever, and your chances of even getting an answer from either are probably no more than 1 in 1,000. (You can build the odds against you to more like 1 in 5,000 if you throw in a few misspelled words too.)

No matter where you start out, be it from that transformed bedroom-into-an-office-at-home now that little Greg is off to college, a basement office, a renovated one half of your 2-car garage after deciding that the Volkswagen can now be consigned to standing in the driveway, nobody thousands of miles away is going to know just how small an operator you are. Therefore, Step #1 is to get a *magnificent looking* letterhead. Note, we did not say cheap, average, we did not say better-than-average. We said get a *magnificent looking* letterhead. If white, on the finest grade, high rag-content paper available! Or, consider pastels, with matching envelopes. Don't worry too much about elaborate design. If your letterhead is engraved, embossed, or otherwise made to look very expensive, a simple, sharp, clean design should suffice. And, if spelling gives you difficulties, your very next acquisition should be a good dictionary. You cannot afford to misspell words. This slight fault alone can cost you thousands and thousands of dollars in *lost* finders' fees.

What to put on your glorious letterhead? Simple rule is *to make your service sound as broad-based as you can possibly make it sound.* Saliently, if you were to have printed, "John Jones,

Shoestring Finder," it would be difficult for the seller of California Redwood Patio Rounds to understand why you were contacting him. If you're not incorporated, something like "Jones Business Service" is an all-encompassing title that allows you to operate in almost any field. If you've got good all-around management experience, the words, "Management Consultant," after your name will impress many businessmen. "Business Consultant," too, is good. "Advertising and Promotion Services," albeit you're restricted somewhat, is not bad. But, we've found it best *not* to use the words, "Finder's Service." Too many Businessmen, predominantly those who advertise such fee offers, for too many years have been hit up by Finders pressing them for fees in exchange for a name provided from a directory. Habitually, their letters are on poor quality paper (even post cards) and loaded with many misspelled words, creating the conception, in the mind of the Businessman, that he's contending with an illiterate. Thus, the word "Finder" has become anathema to many Businessmen. Unfair? Perhaps. Because that is what you are *actually* serving as: a Finder! But, if the old saying "If you can't lick 'em, join 'em," must prevail, then go *with* the tide. Don't try to buck it. Even though you're dealing in pure Finders' fees, if these are referred to as promotion fees, advertising fees, service fees, consultant's fees—nearly anything else—you can anticipate a better hearing, a better chance for success.

At this point it should be evident that you also need a good, clean-faced typewriter. If you can't type, and your wife, girl friend, mistress, or whomever else close to you *also* can't type, *learn*. Or, "hunt and peck." But, *under no circumstances* send out letters on your beautiful stationery hand-written. If you don't have a typewriter you can pick up a decent used one, usually for around $150.00.

O. K. Now you've got that spare room in which to operate (that portion of your home used for business wholly tax-deductible if you rent—deductible to the extent of utilities expenses if you own—by the way). You have $150.00 worth of typewriter. You have some $30.00 worth of letterheads that will make recipients want to run their fingers over the paper just because of its elegance. And, you have a good dictionary. All of your beginning product, source and reference information you can get from your public library; so that's free.

How else can you get into any universal, world-wide business on an initial investment of under $200.00?

Now you're ready to start investigating the various fields in which you can operate as a Finder at maximum profit. This brings us logically to Chapter 3.

CHAPTER 3

What Are the Most Lucrative Fields?

As, MORE AND MORE, the monetary balance of this country shifts (always toward the worse) people, more and more, are putting greater and greater emphasis on acquiring tangible "things." Investors, disgusted and fed up with dollar devaluations, trade imbalances, and ever-constant inflation, are, too, turning to *tangibles* of all sorts.

Hence, in keeping with the public mood, let's start out in this direction.

COMMODITIES & MINERALS

Canned foods of all kinds, because of their natural preservation qualities, make up a consistently good market. Scrap steel is growing as a market (even to the point where we recently had a Subscriber offering Finders' fees for all the railroad steel he could buy). As of early 1972 platinum was enjoying a big demand, probably because it is one of the best catalysts for anti-pollution devices. Mercury remains strong in demand, it seems, right through the ups and downs of such metals as lead, zinc and copper. Nickel, overall, enjoys strong demand. Although it's illegal for U. S. citizens to own gold, some Finders make big money, parlaying its intrinsic value with foreign Central Bankers' flip-flop decisions on how to relate it to their currencies. Silver, temporarily down, has a brilliant long-range future, if for no other reason than its indispensability to the giant photographic industry alone.

How do you start in commodities and minerals? The same way you'd start in anything else: through *knowledge*. The New York Mercantile Exchange has a veritable gold mine of information (most of it free, some costing $1.00 or less). And, the American Association of Commodity Traders is also a good source. For pure commodities—pork bellies, corn, wheat, etc., check your local library for the trade associations and Chicago Exchange addresses in this field. We've also seen several Finders make big sums through dealings in cement—that's right, plain old cement. Energy fuels such as crude oils, butane and propane don't have to play second best to anyone in world markets—thus making for huge profit potentials for the Finder. You can even make money in Bee-Hive coke, believe it or not. Others, too numerous to mention, make up a vast sea (and much of your finding in minerals and commodities will be dealing in shipments moving across seas) of quick, windfall profits for the alert Finder.

PRECIOUS & SEMI-PRECIOUS STONES

"Diamonds Are Forever" is the apropos title of one of the James Bond adventure novels written by the late Ian Fleming. He was right. They are. Even with the onslaught of the new, supposedly perfectly chemically compounded "man-made diamonds," nothing can compare with the laser-like flash of brilliance that hits you in the eye when light strikes a *real* diamond in just the right way. Despite the world's short supply, limited to South Africa in any quantity, this is a good field to deal in as a Finder. Opals, which have been appreciating steadily in value at a rate of 10%-15% per year, in recent years, is another of the precious and semi-precious stones markets well worth looking into. And, naturally, emeralds and rubies will never have to take a back seat to anything.

When you get into *semi*-precious stones, however, you are perhaps getting into the biggest volume, fastest turnover market in this category. Reason: *mass-market* . . . after all, how big a percentage of the population of *any* country can afford diamonds, emeralds or rubies?

Big markets, and much bigger every year, are developing in jade, tiger eyes (from Taiwan), garnet, smoky quartz, topaz and tourmaline. Of course, genuine (blue, rough) Persian turquoise is always in big demand, selling as high as $15.00 a carat. But native U. S. turquoise, found mostly around the copper mines of Arizona, is frequently smuggled out for a reason: *fast-growing demand.*

The sharp Finder can make *millions of dollars* in this field alone.

SURPLUS & CLOSE-OUT MERCHANDISE

Goofs, goofs, goofs! American industry seems to become more capable of production line ineptness, and *needless overproduction,* each year. The inevitable result is a massive outpouring of goods, products and merchandise of every description that cannot be sold through standard wholesaler/retailer channels at standard retail prices.

Example (and this happens, oh, so often): The Butterfingers

Mfg. Co. is sold by a fast-talking business promoter into setting up a new subsidiary to manufacture a "sure-fire-seller" combination pen knife, can opener, eye liner and dynamic tension spring device. Butterfingers goes hog wild on the "scientific" market research premise that the wife of the company's president liked the idea . . . so did her Aunt Effie and Uncle Amos. A production line is set up. Costs are figured at Xc per unit, wholesale prices at XXc, and retail prices at XXXXc. Production roars ahead, because the cost accounting department tells production that the device must be mass-produced in order to keep the cost-per-unit down. Then the buck is passed to the marketing department with the word that, "we're stocked to our teeth with this new product, so you can guarantee instant delivery on all sales." Marketing, in turn, finds out in a hurry that quick delivery is *not* going to be the problem—that getting rid of a huge inventory *is* going to be the problem. Thus, comes onto the market a huge overstock of a new product that the Butterfingers Mfg. Co. would like only to get its tooling costs back on . . . or practically give them away if they can't do that, in order to get a tax write-off.

Enter the Finder. He has uncovered a marketing firm in Mexico which has found that there is nothing more in this world that Mexican women want than a combination pen knife, can opener, eye liner and dynamic tension spring device. He unloads for Butterfingers and collects a fat fee.

Now this is what can only be called an *extreme* example. We don't *really* believe *anybody* could make money on such a product. But, at least you can follow our recounting of how many overstocks are made, and big bargains in "surplus" and close-out merchandise occur.

In 1969 we had a subscriber firm, one of the biggest marketing and merchandising firms in the world, which offered 10% Finders' fees for finding carload (minimum) quantities of *any* product. The Firm had "dumping" outlets all over the world. Many of our subscribers made a good deal of money *working for this firm alone.*

NEW PRODUCTS

They're everywhere. A lot of good ones too. Overseas manufacturers of all kinds are constantly and literally crying to break into the American Market. And the reverse is also true: U. S. manufacturers of all kinds are constantly and literally crying to break into overseas markets. So . . . why not put 'em together (contacts with each other, that is) and collect a bunch of worthwhile Finders' fees for yourself? Information? It's everywhere too. The *Thomas Register* is a basic reference work that depicts and describes the production and product types of just about all of American Industry. Your public library has all sorts of other such reference works in addition to trade magazines in various fields, and some of the bigger libraries also stock overseas magazines and directories.

INVENTIONS

One of the biggest hoaxes perpetrated on the American public today is that a patent means all-out protection for the patent holder, and that he will become wealthy himself if he only shows patience, forces the big corporation to come to him, hat in hand, and beg him for the use of his patent in return for a juicy royalty contract.

Hogwash!

Big corporations all have staffs of patent attorneys and research and development engineers geared solely to the purpose of "inventing around" any patient they think might make a valuable addition to their line and avoid the on-into-infinity expense of paying royalty checks to the original inventor. Unless you have a so-called "basic" patent, e.g., a self-locking device with but one moving part, your chances of getting a royalty deal with a big corporation are about as good as was George McGovern's winning the presidential race of 1972. Most big Corporations need more hard-headed you-can-use-it-if-you'll-pay-me-and-my-heirs-a-fortune-in-royalties-forever proposals like Custer needed more Indians.

However—and this is an important however—there is another side to the coin. When pursued properly, inventions *can* be sold. And the best way is outright. Thus, the knowledgeable Finder, in aiding the Inventor (who is often strong in engineering talent, weak in marketing talent), can frequently earn good Finders' fees by helping the inventor *sell outright* his invention.

Look at it from the corporation's side. It has stockholders to account to for (immediate) profits. It has accounting red tape up to its eyelids (this is why it doesn't want to add anything at all to its fixed long-term obligation ledgers). *But*—and this is an important but—it *also* has its marketing, sales, and sometimes its advertising departments pushing it to get a quick good deal on a new product that would be a perfect complement to its line. Therefore, it's the outright cash sale of an invention that appears to be the very best avenue to take.

Where do you get information on patents? First, inventors are everywhere. Through friends and associates you can smoke a lot of them out. Second, you can get all the information you want on new inventions directly from the U. S. Patent Office, Washington, D. C. And, if in doubt, back to your public library, the best and most complete informational source you can use for researching *any* subject.

(We believe the common misconception that manufacturers everywhere are head-over-heels eager to make long-term royalty deals with inventors stemmed, originally, from the practice of book publishers of making royalty payments to authors. Here, the situation is entirely different, simply because the book publisher wishes to assure a steady flow of new work from authors whose work he thinks he can sell. This is but a "throw-in" observation . . . not really valid to a discussion of *inventors'* royalties.)

COLLECTORS' ITEMS & ANTIQUES

So much has been said about coins that we will hastily gloss over this subject and get on to other things. When the U. S. Treasury—a non-profit organization—can earn a profit of $18 million on its first sale of Eisenhower silver dollar mint sets, well . . . nuff said.

There are many other collectors' items of undeterminable value wasting away in attics and basements throughout the U. S. A newspaper reporting the assassination of Lincoln, Teddy Roosevelt's charge up San Juan Hill, the beginning of our entry into World War I or II, a wrong headline covering an important event . . . Postage Stamps of high denomination, or very limited press runs in the classification of commemoratives (like the 1948 series), or of archaic age . . . Any kind of product made out of a special kind of material, or with a special kind of skill, now extinct . . . these are the elements that make up a Finder's paradise. Despite the high rate of transience of the American public, *treasures in truck and trash* are everywhere. (Author's note: at the tender age of 23, we made $18,000 in Finders' fees over a 1-year period while attending college by uncovering just such items, and selling them at big profits for their owners. That was a heap of money way back in them thar days.)

And, how about antiques? What can be said as to the intrinsic value of an 1860 rolltop desk, imported hand-carved furniture from the Victorian era, firearms of the Wild Bill Hickok age back to the days of Andy Jackson. We'd bet you could walk down any street in any *old section* (pre-1915 built homes) in just about any city, and, if allowed to enter and examine the contents of attic and basement, you'd find a *small fortune* in valuables of which the owner did not even know the worth in at least one out of every seventy-five homes (a very high ratio).

Suggestion: Place classified ads in such magazines and newspapers as *GRIT, CAPPERS WEEKLY,* and the many farm periodicals. Reason? *You'll want to reach the old homestead market.* Copy would read something like this:

> A FORTUNE IN YOUR ATTIC?
> Send whatever you've accumulated for generations—over 100 years old—for our appraisal. Send insured, with return postage & extra $ to assure safe return in case of rejection. If accepted, we will work on a 20% sales commission in getting the very top market price for you.
> YOU MAY BE WEALTHY AND NOT EVEN KNOW IT. Get full free details.

If you can get the words "fully bonded" into the ad, so much the better. It will inspire much more confidence.

(Incidentally, this is roughly the same approach we used many years ago. If you decide to try it, we think it best to buy a periscope and an oxygen tank so that you can breath while you're peering over the stack of packages you'll receive.)

REAL ESTATE & FINANCING

Here is one of the juiciest and *biggest paying* areas of the entire Finders' fee arena. Many, many, many men have hauled in fees of $100,000 to $1,000,000 and more on *single* transactions such as the purchase, sale or financing of large shopping centers, industrial complexes, high-rise apartments and office buildings, and 100,000-acre-plus ranches, to name but a few. Sour note here, though: Through the complete discombobulation and lack of any standards in the various states' laws concerning Finders' activities in these areas, you must tread with great caution. Example: The states of Texas and California have laws stating that anyone in another state who is not a licensed real estate broker cannot be paid a Finder's fee if he is not a licensed real estate broker in his home state. The state of Florida has a separate examination for a mortgage broker's license. In some states a real estate broker's license automatically enables him to deal in mortgages and business brokerage too. In other states, real estate brokerage and business brokerage are considered separate.

Net result of all this confusion in the disparate state laws is that the Finder must tread *very lightly*—he cannot insert himself directly into the middle of negotiations between two parties and act as an intermediary (as he *can* do in most other areas of finding). He must have enough sense to get the two parties together, *then back off and let them work out all the details of the agreement together with their own attorneys, accountants and/or licensed brokers.* Under no circumstances, in these fields, can a Finder act as a direct intermediary if he is not licensed.

We've found that this "rap" is relatively easy to beat, though . . . through this simple means: *Get the appropriate license.* In some states getting a real estate broker's license can be tough, calling for one to two day examinations. In many other states it's much easier. (Several years ago we obtained a real estate broker's license in Wisconsin, one of the tougher states in which to do this, merely by reading a book preparatory to the exam.) Moral: *Get yourself a real estate broker's license if you wish to "cash-in" in many of these areas . . . other licenses for other areas.*

Another step, easier yet, is to tie-in with a broker by taking the real estate *salesman's* examination. In just about every state in the Union this can be done more simply than going through the rigors of getting a *broker's* license.

Much information—books, courses, etc.—will offer you a complete real estate course, for X number of dollars. Some of these can be helpful, but the value of real estate education lies in application of it to the state in which you reside, for all your actions will be covered by the laws of your own community. Therefore, we'd think the first step in this direction *would be to contact your own local real estate exchange.* This body can point you in the right direction, point out the proper study and informational materials to acquire. One point to remember when dealing with any real estate body: Politics is often involved; the exchanges are made up of real estate men. It is not unknown for a real estate exchange, upon getting a request from a person for information on how to become a broker or salesman, to react, inwardly, with the thought, "Oh, oh, more competition!" If you are careful to point out in your request that you do *not* intend to set up a full-fledged real estate office, but only wish to get the license to enable you to dabble in a few cross-country deals (if you mention "on the side," better yet), you'll probably get more full, eager and helpful information and cooperation.

Just within the past five years we've seen fees of $150,000, $122,000, $118,000, $100,000, $105,000 and $102,000 earned on the sale of apartment houses. We've learned of a fee as high as

$1,700,000 on the sale of an industrial complex. One man in 1965 earned $2,500,000 on the sale of a large mining property. Fees of $40,000 to $100,000 are common on all kinds of real estate and financing deals. And, those going as high as $3,000,000 are not unheard of.

Worth the effort of becoming a real estate broker or salesman?

MERGERS & ACQUISITIONS

Sol S. was a self-admitted introvert. He worked in the back room of a Wall Street Securities House, and longed for a much better life for his wife and five kids than his $15,000 a year income could provide. So, Sol, knowing the Great Secret, joined many country and athletic clubs in the greater New York area. His total dues must have run equal to his yearly securities house earnings. He mortgaged everything he had in 1964 in order to impress the top social set of New York with his own "high" social status, merely to get access to the ears of some of the country's top Businessmen. Sol smelled the coming merger/acquisition boom abuilding, and wanted badly to cash-in. *He did* . . . and in a very *big* way. Early in 1966, he told us he'd quit his job with the securities house because his earnings in 1965, through bringing merger and acquisition parties together, totalled some *twenty-five times* his annual salary. He told us he never earned less than $100,000 on any single merger, and that he collected on several a year. (Unfortunately, right after that long phone conversation, we had a near fatal car accident, spent a year in the hospital, and never heard from Sol again. Presumably he's long since retired, perhaps living like a king in Bermuda.)

In the brief success story of Sol we mentioned the Great Secret. What's this? The Secret that can turn any shy introvert into a charming, warm, engaging personality, the kind of person whom anybody from a common, everyday Businessman, to an elderly Spinster would trust with their life savings?

Interest . . . in the other guy!

Perhaps the forced approach to a stranger, with a lot of idle talk about how well his shirt and tie go together, combined with the well-styled hair cut complete with salt and pepper flecks, giving him the appearance of a foreign diplomat, is a bit phony. But it will work better than 75% of the time. The conversation—*all about the other guy*—can easily grow from such humble beginnings to what his wife is like, what his favorite sports and hobbies are, to where his kids are attending college. The startling part of this approach, though, *is that in many cases the forced approach will develop into genuine interest in the other guy and lead to a long and lasting friendship.*

If any such overwhelmingly complex subject can be oversimplified, this is the real meaning of what all the inspirational courses, books, magazines, seminars, and the like, try to get across: We all live on a small planet—3.5 billion astronauts, sailing continuously around the sun. So, why not make the most of it. . . and it's *other* people, and the amount of your own introspection you can get rid of by wrapping yourself up in *their* problems, that can put *real meaning* into your life.

Of course, Sol's objective was personal financial gain. But, in the process of becoming a self-made millionaire, *he won hundreds of true-blue-loyal friends too* . . . a thundering "human relations" bonus! Even a man who blamed Sol for a merger that ultimately didn't work out to his liking told us once, ". . . but how could you ever get mad at a guy like that."

In the first chapter of our book, *THE ENCYCLOPEDIA OF LITTLE-KNOWN, HIGHLY PROFITABLE BUSINESS OPPORTUNITIES* (Fell), on Finders' fees, we advocated intimate relationships—all you can manage—with influential Businessmen *in your own local community.* Then *match* these precious contacts with others you will cultivate by correspondence many miles away. We think the illustration just given shows how the "forced interest" beginning can be made. Although the "forced interest" approach is more difficult in correspondence, it can be done here, too. In Chapter 4 we'll explain.

In the field of mergers and acquisitions, as in the field we just discussed—real estate and financing—you have pretty much the same problems with licensing. If you are *not* a securities broker/dealer, get the parties together, *then get out of their way*. You *cannot*, without a license, act as an actual intermediary. The problem is much like that of the hospital that will not permit a veterinarian to take out your wife's gall bladder. Maybe he could do as good a job as an M. D. because a certain animal has a gall bladder in the same place. But the hospital will not allow him to do the actual surgery because he is not *specifically licensed* to ply his talents on humans. So, again, in this section we must emphasize the importance of not getting into any document signing yourself having to do with the transfer of assets, real property and financing. It's best not even to put your name to any of the physical transferral papers, even as a witness.

Now that we've talked about the disadvantages of acting as a Finder in the fields of real estate, financing, mergers and acquisitions, let's point out one big advantage: Unlike commodities, minerals, precious stones, surplus and close-out merchandise, new products, collectors' items and antiques, there is always a *public record* of major real estate, financing, merger and acquisition deals. Hence you can always protect yourself, learn the specifics, exact data, and the time the transaction was concluded, so that nobody can cheat you out of your fee by the art of simple silence.

A BUNCH OF OTHER POSSIBILITIES

Independent manufacturers' representatives throughout the country are constantly looking for new products to complement their lines. Once you have built adequate cross-reference files from several of the other major categories you will have the "raw meat" match-ups with which to approach them. The *MANUFACTURER'S AGENT'S GUIDE* lists more than 11,000 manufacturers representatives in the U. S. and Canada.

To a lesser extent, the same holds true for Wholesalers. While most will only accept big-volume, name-brand merchandise, occasionally some will be interested in big "good deal" close-outs.

Chef Choate's Navajo Bread would be of no interest to those living on the Reservation, because most Navajos make this delicious food themselves. But, his compilation of exotic and nutritious Navajo recipes could conceivably be a big seller east of the Mississippi, along the Pacific Coast, and all major metropolitan centers where most people of the fast-growing, health-food-conscious set could be interested. We could see where an alert Finder, introducing these "different" concoctions to large wholesale bakeries in these areas could possibly make a "kill" in fees.

Custom manufacturing is still another area to exploit. We've run a few ads in *BUSINESS OPPORTUNITIES DIGEST* in the past from a variety of manufacturers offering Finders' fees for those finding users for their facilities—ranging from cosmetics compounding and packaging, to laminating, to structural steel fabrication, and just about every other type of manufacturing, engineering and warehousing help in between. The classified section of the Sunday *New York Times,* under "Manufacturing Facilities Offered" is an especially good source of leads here.

Specialty mail order companies—particularly the catalog houses

—are always on the lookout for new products. Why not consider this field? It's enormous—from the hundreds of national firms that put out little 16-64-page catalogs to the giants like Sears, Montgomery Ward, Alden's and Spiegel's.

In all, through much reading and study of trade, business and specialty magazines, sparks of "put-together" possibilities that can pay you lush Finders' fees can ignite and go off like fireworks in your head.

CHAPTER 4

Setting Up a Finders' Business

IN CHAPTER 2 we talked of the embryonics—a room, typewriter, a beautiful letterhead.

Now, let us suppose that your pile of "feeling-out" correspondence is beginning to grow. It then becomes time consuming to make an important decision. This correspondence will give you some automatic market research "direction."

In what areas—commodities, minerals, gems, surplus merchandise, new products, inventions, imports, exports, collectors' items, antiques, real estate, financing, mergers, other—did you seem to make the best "first impact?" It's probably best to *specialize* in a single specialty, particularly in the beginning. *Learn your first field well.* Start bringing in a few bucks. If you feel your earnings in one field are adequate, stop, and *concentrate* on it. One field alone may be all you'll need. On the other hand, if you're successful in a reasonably short period of time, you may wish to add other fields, *slowly, cautiously, learning each well as you explore.*

WANT TO GO IT ALONE?

If so, your best bets are in commodities, minerals, gems, surplus stocks, new products, inventions, collectors' items and antiques. More intimate tie-ins (with professionals) might be essential in imports and exports because of sticky duty regulations and shipping red-tape . . . not as necessary if you're dealing *only* with importers and exporters in this country. While you can possibly "go it alone" in real estate, financing, mergers and acquisitions, these are the very slowest of slow build-up possibilities for you, because of the intensive study and plodding licensing procuring process which should precede full-scale actions.

WHY NOT SHORT-CUT AND FIGURE LOGICAL "TIE-IN" RELATIONSHIPS?

Attorneys are a "natural" tie-in for *all sorts* of business relationships. Many will work on a contingent fee basis, just as you will be doing as a Finder. And, a key letter, written on an attorney's letterhead, has a greater ring of authority than that written on just about any other kind of stationery. Consider it. Another possibility: If you have a personal friend who is an attorney he will probably work on a retainer basis of only a few dollars a month . . . or, at least, permit you to use his name so that you can refer to "your attorney" by name in your correspondence. The little cc: John Jones, Attorney, at the bottom of your letters can create a solid conviction among recipients that "this guy knows what he's doing." The ring of professionalism cannot be denied.

A close association with an accounting firm can be good in the *buying and selling* of businesses. Here, the authority is implied because of the complex nature of P & Ls, financial statements, assets, book value and net worth.

A good bank relationship is important in the selling of personal property of all kinds—from exports, imports, commodities, minerals, etc., because of the ease and convenience of concluding transactions through bank-to-bank deals—through correspondent banking facilities. (More on this subject later in this chapter.)

Like the "friendly" neighborhood insurance agent, it seems just about everyone knows a "friendly" neighborhood real estate broker. *This is one of the best tie-ins you can get.* As we said earlier, once you obtain a broker's or salesman's license, *you have a relatively free hand to operate in just about any field.*

The one last *good* tie-in that we can think of is a *management consultant.* In fact, this opportunity is *so* good, just wait until you read about all the ramifications of this in Chapter 7. Licensing laws are nil in this field. And, while most work is done on a retainer basis, rather than a contingent fee basis, we see no reason why an *excellent* relationship cannot be built up between you and one. Naturally, if General Foods is going to consider hiring a management consultant, they are going to engage someone like Booz, Allen & Hamilton, George Fry and Associates, or McKinsey and Co. Here you would be out in the snow. But, look at it this way: There are more than 15,000 college professors in the U. S. who work as management consultants on the side. In addition, there are God-only-knows how many little one and two man operations in this field.

We'll now repeat a point we made in the last paragraph, because it's so important: In Chapter 7 we'll tell you all about the *dynamic, make-money-in-all-directions potential* through such a relationship.

USE PSYCHOLOGY

Whichever way you decide to jump—going it alone, or tying-in with someone else—we're assuming you've now "felt-out" various markets and fields and are now ready to "swing." Continue on by *refining and shortening* your letters. After all, you'll be dealing wih many influential Businessmen and Executives who have little time for developing pen pal relationships; they're too busy making money. And, they can make it for you, too, if you play your cards right, all faces up.

Write friendly, but short, crisp, businesslike, direct-to-the-point letters. You'll get more respect for it, *and you'll be able to work in psychology, too.*

If your letter writing style is vintage of the 1890s, and goes something like the following, well . . . either take an exhaustive course in business letter writing, or get out of the Finders' business.

How *not* to write a business letter:

Dear ________________:

Please be advised that I have an intimate contact who controls the 300,000 tons of #1 scrap steel in which you've indicated interest. As I've told you about him before, I think it would be wise to cooperate, as his interest in selling to you may decline. Upon notification and firm confirmation of my fee from you, which I've already asked you for several times, I shall proceed to arrange the proper introductions, the hardships put upon me by the trauma of the complications and reservations made by you, needlessly postponing the consummation of this business transaction, not withstanding. I shall expect a prompt reply from you.

Now let's turn it around. If you can write a short letter, 20th century style, something like this, you just might end up with a completed deal and a whopping Finders' fee to bank:

Dear ________________:

Whew! It was rough, but I think I've made it. Believe I've got you the seller. Good Joe, this guy! He wants to meet you, and I think you can wrap up in a hurry now. By the way, full specs on the 300,000 tons of #1 scrap steel are enclosed again. Just want to be sure you've got it again, in case you want to double-check. We've already worked out the details on my fee. I'm satisfied. Know your boss is going to be happy as a little kid on his first visit to a 3-ring circus if we can push this deal through. And, the very day it happens, you'd better skip breakfast and lunch, 'cause

I'm going to fly to Cleveland and buy you the biggest, melt-in-your-mouth filet in town for dinner. Let's keep our fingers crossed, George.

GETTING THE BALL ROLLING

The foregoing letter examples we were giving under the assumption of a business sale that was well along—heading into the final stages of completion. They were presented only as, what we believe to be, proper and improper psychology.

Now, let's back track for the moment and trace how to get started, *with total strangers,* with people you've never sent a letter to yet, with people who, if you don't grab their interest right off, may regard your letter with as much interest as a Lon Chaney film festival.

First, obviously, try employing some of the *personal*-contact Great Secret strategies of Sol S. Get together a dozen or so specifications of the "wants" and "availabilities" of leading Businessmen in your *own* community . . . then start looking, via letter, long distance.

How?

Learn your markets! Before you can write even your *first* letter, this should be a self-evident truism.

1. Get a flying start through the reference, directory and "how-to" informational materials available to you *through your public library.*

2. Pick up copies of and/or subscribe to the *basic* daily newspapers in the business field, *THE WALL STREET JOURNAL* and *THE JOURNAL of COMMERCE* (N. Y.). Each is jam-packed with current, up-to-the-minute market data, prices, statistics and figures of every sort. In other, more specialized fields, read such magazines as *SALESMAN'S OPPORTUNITY, THE*

MINING JOURNAL, INCOME OPPORTUNITIES, SUCCESS UNLIMITED, THE ANTIQUE TRADER, HOBBIES, MONEY MAKING OPPORTUNITIES, THE COIN COLLECTOR, AGENCY SALES (the magazine for manufacturers reps) and *OPPORTUNITY MAGAZINE*. Most of these are available in libraries or at your newsstand.

3. "Bone up" on your first area of specialty by reading five to fifteen *books* which cover that field in all of its ramifications.

Now . . . *you are ready to start sending out your first letters.* A few examples, involving hypothetical situations:

Dear ________________ :

A local wholesaler is looking for a big supply of (super-duper, space age widgets). I saw your ad in the SURPLUS REVIEW, *and wondered if you can supply these.*

Let me know, and I'll give you full information.

Dear ________________ :

Just last week I came across a Smithsonian Institution "Patron Series" set—twelve books in mint condition, copyright 1925. I understand only fifteen sets were published that year. And, I figured you, being one of the most reputable of all the New York rare book dealers, might be interested. Am I right?

Dear ________________ :

A big real estate developer here has got an option on one of the juiciest, high-traffic-area land parcels you could ever believe. He wants to put a big shopping center on it, and has only 60 days to exercise the option, or lose out. He's overextended—has several big high-profit jobs going—and has got to come up with some interim financing soon, in order to cash-in on this golden opportunity.

He needs about $2,000,000, and is real flexible on terms. Interested? If so, I'll tell you a lot more.

Dear ________________ :

A Prominent Australian Businessman has a source of wool, selling some 20% under *the market price reported in last Friday's edition of* THE JOURNAL OF COMMERCE. *(Note: you always* assume *that the recipient stays "up" on all facets of business, economics and markets.)*

If you're interested, let me know and I'll send you the eye-opening details.

Important note: From the content of these sample letters, under the *generalized* title of your business (see Chapter 2), the recipient has no ideas what your role in the deal is. He doesn't know whether you're an agent, broker, dealer, finder, business associate of the principal of some kind, or simply a close friend of the other-end contact. Fine. *Let him guess.* It's to your advantage in the beginning. At this state, *all you want is to get some communication going.* And, you may get it from the curiosity standpoint alone—a reply for the sake of his wanting to know what your part in the deal is.

Three *additional* things you can do that should *increase* your response percentage are these:

1. Center your short letter *high* on the letter paper, leaving plenty of blank space at the bottom. Then add, on the bottom line of your high-set letter, something to the effect, "For speed and convenience, why not just write your answer below and return this whole thing to me."
2. Get a supply of the carbonized speed memos (the kind where you type your message on the left-hand or upper side,

and, hopefully, your reply will come back to you on the right-hand or bottom side.)

3. Enclose a business reply envelope.

If you were representing, for instance, an inventor who had a hot idea for a new, low-cost pollution control device, and you addressed your letter simply to "General Motors Corporation," your chances of getting a reply would probably be more like .200 of 1%, rather than the generally expected 2% to 5%. Giant corporations have a habit of routing their mail to the wrong department, where letters that do not apply directly to a particular executive's function end up in his waste basket. After all, who are you? He wants to do a good job for the company in, say, the inventory control department, his realm; he couldn't care less about an engineering proposal. That's the responsibility of the research and development department.

So . . . first and foremost, you've got to determine *to whom* in the company your letter should be addressed.

Obviously, a *name* is by far the best.

Second, a *job title*—such as Marketing Manager, Purchasing Department Manager, Engineering Department Manager, New Product Development Manager, Real Estate Department Manager, Market Research Manager, et. al.—will most frequently get your letter steered through the jungle of corporate internal mail routing into the hands of the person (or his secretary or assistant) you wish to reach.

ROLL THE BALL FURTHER—USE ALL THE LEVERAGE YOU CAN MUSTER

In the 1950s we bought ten shares of stock at $10.00 per share, in a (public) toy manufacturing company. We had no interest in the stock, from the investment viewpoint; we had only a selfish motive—to use it as a form of *leverage.* We represented, as a Finder, a tiny company which controlled a basic patent, with just one moving part, and could see a "can't miss" application of this patent to the toy company's line.

While we can't recall the letter—not having kept the carbon —we can only reconstruct it from memory. The letter (on gorgeous, die-cut, engraved stationery), addressed to the New Product Development Manager, by title, with a carbon copy to the President of the company, went something like this:

Dear Sir:

Being a stockholder, I'm naturally interested in the welfare of _______ Co.

I've come across a basic patent that I feel could revolutionize a major part of our line. (Author's note: We used the words, "our" line, not "your" line. We then went on to give some brief, hard selling description of the patent, and ended up by saying we thought our *acquisition of such a patent could substantially cut* our *costs, and thus substantially contribute to* our *profits.)*

The results were unbelievable. We got back a prompt reply from the New Product Development Manager (carbon copy to the President) wanting to know how to get in touch, *immediately,* with the head of the tiny company. A few days later came a letter from the President of the toy company telling us how pleased he was that the company had such fine stockholder interest, and, naturally, because *our* company was so progressive, it *always* wished to investigate possible applicable new patents, *especially* those suggested by stockholders, and that they were going to do this on my specific suggestion immediately. And, within the next 60 days came letters from the Public Relations Manager (Wasn't it wonderful that the company had such spirited stockholders who would take the time to contribute to the company's welfare), the Sales Manager (The patent sounded like it could absolutely boom company sales), and the Advertising Manager (Sensational, can hardly wait to start promoting).

Negotiations got down to the final stages, when a few small technical details developed. And, when the President and Executive Vice President of the tiny company suddenly became unavailable to straighten them out—they were prone to getting together for frequent martini-drinking parties in strange places, rather than attending to business—the whole thing fell through.

Naturally, we were frustrated; a $24,000 Finder's fee fell out of our pocket. (We sold the $100 worth of toy company stock a year later, though, for $150 after brokerage commissions . . . so, the thing wasn't a total loss.)

Main point we're trying to get across is the tremendous leverage—direct or implied—you can achieve through a letter.

Another example:

In the early fall of 1957, we created an "Institute." Together with another man with a common name acceptable to Archie Bunkers everywhere, we incorporated the "Institute" and had the most beautiful die-cut, engraved stationery you could ever believe printed.

Purpose of the "Institute?"

Nothing . . . concrete, that is . . . it's only purpose was to experiment with what could be done with the power of letters, plus some other miscellaneous and sundry market research.

As all the economists were predicting at that time, we were moving into the severe 1958 recession, and a sick trade magazine needed help. It's advertising lineage had been dropping steadily for four years, and the company was at that time operating at a $400,000 loss.

We gathered together all its competitor's magazines, and wrote to all of their respective advertisers—a total of some 150 letters. All were brief, went out over the common name, "Executive Director" of the "Institute" and went something like this:

Dear ________________ :

Noted your ad in ___*(magazine)*___ *. You are to be congratulated for keeping a good advertising campaign going in the face of current business conditions.*

We practically never read the ___*(magazine)*___ *, however. Just by chance we picked up a copy (true). We read regularly, cover-to-cover* ___*(name of magazine we were trying to help—again a true statement)*___ *and wonder why you don't advertise more in this fine publication.*

Yes, the results to this short letter were also phenomenal. Of the some 150 letters we received approximately 75 replies, a fantastic percentage when you consider that *no reply was even solicited*. And, of these 75 replies, about 98% were bubbly, warm, charming, in every way favorable.

Result?

In the recession year of 1958, the magazine we were trying to help *more than doubled* its advertising lineage, and showed a $600,000 profit . . . a turn-around of $1,000,000 from the previous year's $400,000 loss.

Devious?

A bit! The clear inference in our letter to the toy company was that we were a *major* stockholder in their firm. If the various company executives knew that we only held $100.00 worth of stock in their multi-million dollar company, they may have been, shall we say, slightly miffed. But, with brokerage house street name accounts, how could they know? We *could* have been gathering their stock in huge blocks, either individually, or as the head of a syndicate, and been considering a proxy or take-over battle if they didn't look over the patent. We bought the stock only to salve our conscience—so that we could honestly say we were a stockholder of their company. In the case of the letters to the advertisers, all we did was tell the plain, unvarnished truth. Apparently, because the advertisers were unused to getting letters complimenting them on their advertising, on a letterhead that looked like antique parchment, and signed by a man who sounded like he was a true Captain of Industry, the *leverage* in their choice of media in which to advertise in 1958 was applied to its fullest.

We think these are two classic examples of how *leverage* can be made to work for you. And, luckily, in all walks of business, there are virtually limitless possibilities to *use* it. A little imagination, a little implication, a little innuendo can do wonders in the reception you'll get. You'll be *positively amazed* at the number of doors that can open *wide* to you.

THIS MATTER OF PROTECTING YOURSELF—THROUGH EXCHANGES OF LETTERS, AGREEMENTS AND CONTRACTS

Now that you've broken the ice, have established some rapport with the parties you are trying to get together, and presumably have discussed terms in previous correspondence and phone calls, your next problem is to get something in writing, from one or the other, committing one or the other to paying you your fee. From the legal standpoint, a clearly worded, concise and specific *exchange of letters* should be sufficient.

With a covering note, saying something like, "I know this letter sounds kind of stiff, but it's a formality—something I must have for my files before we can finalize," you might write this kind of letter:

Dear ________________ :

I think we have now agreed on the terms of my compensation in return for acting on your behalf in finding __(whatever)__ .

It is to be (so many dollars, a one-payment %, payments based upon units of sale—other). Upon your acceptance of these terms, I will reveal the full identities—name(s), address(es), phone number(s)—of the principals—to you, together with the last of the information in my possession, which I have, until now, withheld in order to assure my compensation for services rendered. Further, it is understood that you were not aware of (whatever opportunity) prior to (date of first contact), and that you will protect me for my fee, whether or not you were acquainted with the opposite party in any other way.

Accepted by (signature) Representing (Co.) Date____

As you might expect, one step better, if you can get it, is an *actual contract.*

Many would refer to such a contract as a "Finder's Protection Agreement." We prefer, "Business Service Agreement." Such a contract should read something along this avenue:

I, (name), representing (Co., self, partners, a syndicate, other—should be spelled out), do hereby agree to the following terms of compensation to be paid to (your name) in return for services rendered. These services ________________

____

____

____

(be certain all terms are spelled out in exact detail).

I, (name), agree to hold in strict confidence all information provided, and will interpret these data broadly, to give full effect as to its intent, and not narrowly, in order to avoid its intent.

I have signed no such similar agreement with any other per-

son(s) having anything to do with our specific __(transaction—again, spell out precisely)__

Witness ____________	Signature ____________
Witness ____________	Title ____________
Witness ____________	Co. ____________
	St. Address ____________
Dated this day __(date)__	City & State ____________
of __(month)__ , the year,	
19___	Countersigned:
	Signature ___(yours)___
Witness ___(yours)___	Title ____________
Witness ____________	Co. ____________
Witness ____________	St. Address ____________
	City & State ____________

A minimum of two copies must be made—one for you, and one for your principal. Not being an attorney, obviously we cannot do as good a job in designing a form that will protect you down to the last period and comma. So if you really want to do up the contract form "right," *by all means consult an attorney.*

Some greedy, unwilling-to-work Finders will sometimes try to "get into the act." They will claim that by merely providing a name *they* are entitled to the fee. This is why the last paragraph in the contract form is so important. Generally speaking, if another Finder has provided only a name, and performed no other services, he does not, legally, have as much as a balloon of air to stand on. The courts still (generally) consider the rule of "value given for value received." Also, most frequently, *prior dates* on correspondence will protect you and your principal from the professional suit-threatener, do-nothing, Johnny-come-lately Finder.

THIS MATTER OF BANK CONFIRMATIONS

Good banking connections are vital to many areas of professional finding. One of your first orders of business is to establish them. Talk to your banker. Make up some mythical transactions as examples. Get his opinion on the best ways to deal—with this kind of assurance, bank confirmations, behind you. If you're not satisfied with what you're told, see another banker, maybe still another, maybe a dozen or even more. Compare notes. Then do business with the bank that seems to know, most, what it's talking about.

CHAPTER 5

Necessary Office Supplies and Equipment

ONE BALMY SPRING DAY in Chicago, in 1963, we visited the shabby office of a Finder who, for ten consecutive years had earned an average income in excess of $100,000 annually—*from the finding business alone.* His office was such a slum-looking pile of debris that we thought this had to be the spot where Mrs. O'Leary's cow started the famous historical blaze.

His "thing" was commodities. His method of operation was atrocious. Beneath and between huge stacks of worn-out books, directories, magazines and paper, piled everywhere, around and on top of his desk, on chairs and the floor, were his "records"—notes scrawled on the backs of envelopes, on lined tablet paper, on the backs of business cards. We even saw one scribbled on a piece of toilet tissue. All were as clear as a doctor's prescription. He even admitted that he shouldn't bother with the notes, because he wrote so fast he couldn't even read half of them anyway.

What saved him, made him an effective, big-money-making Finder, was his photographic mind. *He had total recall.* When we asked him why he never kept carbons of the routine letters he dictated to his part-time secretary, he answered, "What's the sense? I can remember what I said."

Unfortunately, most of us are not human computers. We *need* adequate records, good organization, an efficient system.

At this stage we're assuming you now have a pile of correspondence, some "feelers," a few lucrative possibilities to follow-up. So, *you must next get organized.*

1. You'll need a *subject* card file. Three x five should do, especially if you're specializing in but one field. If you're operating in more than one field, a Kardex or roll-type file could be a bit better.

2. Your subject file should be *cross-referenced* against a *contact* file. Letter files will do while you have relatively few contacts. But, when the number grows over fifty, one hundred, or more, you'll need a quick-access card file, too. You must be able to find out speedily what each contact handles, any credit data you may have, and, if possible, what other Finders he's dealing with (if any).

3. A ledger sheet, kept in chronological order, will tell you at a glance on what date you referred who to whom and other important status information.

Now that you're growing well past the used typewriter, spare room stage, you'll, of course, need tickler and follow-up files, too (we're assuming that you, unlike the Chicago Finder, can't remember everything you said to a hundred different people). And, a weekly "progress report" sheet, ringed into a binder, can serve as a combined budget, running P & L, and sales forecasting device, as well as a market research tool, all rolled into one. (At *BUSINESS OPPORTUNITIES DIGEST* we have just such a simplified one-sheet set-up upon which we can tell the entire state of our business at a glance, and make *major* management decisions within two minutes.) One, set up right, can quickly tell you, via a back flip, where you've been, and where you're going. It can tell you which fields are paying off for you, which are not, and which fields of finding you should consider adding, which fields you should consider dropping.

Other than these things, you'll need the standard items: big desk, trays and/or pigeon hole racks, a coat rack, a letter-size file cabinet . . . and, an extra desk for a beautiful, young, stacked blonde secretary—for occasional monotony-breaking viewing—if you can afford one.

CHAPTER 6

Pitfalls and Pratfalls. What to Do. What to Avoid.

PITFALL #1 is the so-called "daisy chain."

What is a "daisy chain?"

It's simply getting involved with another Finder who is not the direct representative of the Principal but probably claims he is working with another Finder who claims he is. The third Finder, wishing to impress other Finders with his closeness to top principals, may be, in turn, only dealing through a fourth, fifth, sixth, even up to ten, twelve or more other Finders. Once you get sucked into such a web you are starting out on a trip to Nowheresville. The whole thing is a vicious circle: much like the small mail order dealers who "co-publish" all kinds of ad sheets and cheap mimeographed magazines and do nothing but try to sell to each other. In short, you'll end up in a market that is no market; you'll waste your time and money and brain energy senselessly and, 999 times out of every 1,000, fruitlessly.

Figure it. A barrel of crude oil, for instance, can stand an *absolute maximum* of about 3c per barrel in *total* fees added. (This field, crude oil, is one of the *very best* big-money-making areas of the finding business, by the way.) If you're dealing with just one other Finder on such a deal, fine—you'll both pocket a small fortune on, say, a sale of 500,000 barrels at 1½c to you, and 1½c to the other Finder. But, say, for example, a total of eight

Finders are in the act, and all demand ¾c each. Easy to guess: the deal is killed, and nobody gets paid.

Just recently a *BUSINESS OPPORTUNITIES DIGEST* subscriber, a successful Finder for many years, lost out on the biggest deal of his life because he was unwittingly sucked into the "daisy chain." He was the direct representative of a wealthy principal whose estate was overloaded with priceless antiques which he wished to sell. Certainly these antiques were nowhere near the value of the $50,000,000 worth adorning the Hearst Castle at San Simeon, California. Nonetheless, the collection was worth more than a few million.

Another Finder got in touch with him claiming to be the direct representative of a buying principal, which turned out not to be true; he only knew of the buying principal through another Finder. The third Finder, being a particularly clever freeloader, was lying, too, but was most persuasive in his letters and conned the first two into a three-way split of the total 5% sales fee; he then put word out, into the "chain" that he would split his one third with other Finders (the guy didn't want to do any work, just write a few letters and hold his hand out, palm upward, for a fee). Our subscriber, the direct rep Finder of the estate, was flooded with offers and leech-like demands that he pay each of the others a fixed percent of his fee. Somehow, word got out to one *who* the principal was, and the principal, too, was avalanched with such letters, which threw him into a rage.

The result was chaotic. Our subscriber not only lost the opportunity to sell, but also lost the client with whom he'd done much previous business. In a letter to us shortly after the debacle, he sounded like a man who was ready to be fitted with one of those coats with arms that cross and have no outlets for the hands. "I should have known. I should have known. I should have known." This was the babble-essence of his letter.

The "daisy chain" can ruin your various deals in other ways. Many of these Finders, being freeloaders all the way, with a minimum-work, maximum-profit philosophy, will sometimes send you a name and say "try this" (for whatever deal they happened to get wind of that you're working on). Later, if the deal goes through, one will claim that he was vitally instrumental in it, wave his correspondence, send photocopies to you, perhaps threaten suit if you don't split with him. Albeit most often these leeches are about as bothersome as flies lighting on you while you're trying to sleep, you can't always afford to completely ignore the "try this" letter. If and when they come in, the first thing to do is match dates. If the dates on your correspondence precede his, forget it. If there is *any question at all,* reply that you already have been working on it (whatever deal). Quote the *date* that you started, and cite any full authorizations—exchanges of letters or formal contract—that you might have in your possession. This will usually make him back off, and you'll never hear from him again.

On the other hand, sometimes working in the "daisy chain," is the honest, hard working Finder. One rule of thumb, in order to determine how close to the principal he is, is to elicit from him *full details of the requirements.* If he can supply these to you, chances are he's close, perhaps only one other Finder or Broker away from the Principal. A three-way split of a Finders' fee is about the maximum you'll want to go. Obviously, two ways is better, and a *single* fee—yours—is ideal.

When dealing with other Finders it's usually quite easy to separate the men from the boys, however. The professional Finder will be euphonious; he will give elaborate particulars, on good stationery, in a crisp, businesslike way . . . whereas the amateur, or no-work/big-profit leech-type will send you the "try this" letter, too often on shoddy paper with no details (simply because he doesn't have any), or just the few general details he picked up from an ad or a directory.

To sum up: Avoid the "daisy chain" as much as possible. When you must deal with other Finders, and ofttimes this is essential, try to limit the number to three, and no more, on any one transaction.

WHEN TO THREATEN LEGAL ACTION—WHEN NOT TO

O.K. Let's pre-suppose that you worked your fanny off on a juicy Finders' fee deal. You have all your protection agreements, clearly indicating that you are to receive a fee, contingent upon the "closing" of the transaction. You *think* the deal went through, but you don't know for certain. On real estate, financing, merger and acquisition deals you must stay far enough away, if you are not licensed in any way, so that the mystery is greater. In these areas, though, as we've mentioned earlier, your counter-balancing advantage is that *public records* are kept . . . hence a trip to your Register of Deeds or County Clerk's office will quickly tell you if the deal went through. On the other hand, let's say you *believe* a big new products deal you'd been working on went through, but you don't know. Say you live in California, and the deal, if consummated, was in New York. Here is one advantage of being tied in—though very loosely—with a Finders network. You go to your file, pull the name of a New York Finder, write him to check it out on the spot, and if he wishes to do this detective work, you will pay him 15% of your fee—if collected without litigation, or of your net fee (after attorney's costs) if collected with litigation. Another option: Have your attorney write them a letter, *assuming* the deal went through, and that his client (you) will expect his payment shortly. After all, if a long period of silence has ensued since the "closing" of the deal, you can be assured that your principal is trying to cheat you out of your fee. Therefore, a series of "Aw c'mon, I've worked hard on this, I've got bills to pay" letters will probably be ignored. So, why not get right to the point. Better not to mention a law suit in the attorney's letter (the implication is always there in a letter from an attorney, anyway), because, if you're wrong and stumble into ruining some complicated deal *you* could be the victim of a law suit.

In some cases you'll want to maintain relations in a Finder network—mainly for this purpose alone. Finders in business today —good and bad—are more all-encompassing than fleas on a particularly malodorous camel. If they're good for nothing else, at least many are good at routine checking—minor detective work —if they smell the possibility of a, say, $5,000 fee for their limited efforts.

THE FAIR GUY AND THE BULLY

Most often you'll find principals who are glad to pay your fees —*if*, of course, you get the job done for them. It's the same principle that is followed by companies of all sorts—in addition to sales commission rates, the awarding of bonuses, extra incentive gifts and a free top-salesman award of an all expenses paid trip to the Bahamas for you and your wife. *Everybody loves a producer* . . . and will generally pay him promptly and well. The only difference between you and the company setup is that, as a Finder, you are working as an *independent contractor*, so must exercise closer scrutiny upon the closing details of every transaction. More work? Yes. But the rewards are most often *far greater*. (How many salesmen do you know who can pull down $150,000 on a single sale, as a Finder can?)

Therefore, the guys in the white hats outnumber the guys in the black hats by a considerable margin.

But, what do you do when you're confronted by the bully, the guy in the black hat?

Being a Capricorn with a Scorpio rising ourself (if the Zodiac means anything to you), we've always been *fiercely proud*, *fiercely independent, fiercely competitive* and a *fierce fighter.* While many men practice (or try to) the Golden Rule, which simply boils down to treating all men fairly, on kind of a one to one ratio, our philosophy is a little bit different. Due to the *intensity* of our personality, we go more for what should be considered the "eye for an eye" rule—except for the variation that we think, act and practice the *ten* eyes for one rule.

How does this work out in business? We've dealt with many thousands of Businessmen in our first ten years as Editor and Publisher of *BUSINESS OPPORTUNITIES DIGEST,* men who have been honest, fair, polite, hard-working, considerate and kind in every way. For such people we have gone out of our way on a roughly ten to one ratio (value given for value received) to *make* them successful in whatever endeavor was their chosen one. We can proudly say that we've played a very important role in making more than a few men wealthy as a result of this credo.

Now, what happens when that occasional bully comes along? Same ten to one ratio—*but in reverse!* We can best illustrate by two examples, the first from our childhood:

When backed into a corner of our grade school yard—long after school was out one day when we were ten years old—by a bully backed up by five of his "gang," we first learned the Great Lesson of self-preservation—one of *all-out* retaliation.

The pattern always runs something like this: The bully will push you lightly on the shoulder to get your reaction to his threats. If you push him back *equally* as hard, you have a standoff, an unnecessarily complicated shouting match that gets you nowhere. If you push back, *but more lightly,* or, *if you don't push back at all,* chances are great that the bully and his gang will pounce upon you, and you'll end up a badly bruised pulp.

So . . . under such dire circumstances, what alternative do you have? One thing, as we see it (the thing we actually did in the grade school example), at the *first* push of the shoulder you light into the bully with every ounce of strength you've got, you sting him, stun him, smash him, blast his ribs, go for his jugular. . . so that *he* will end up the badly bruised pulp, not you. And when you do this, it's amazing how his gang will back away, make excuses about things they must do, and disperse.

In business, too, there's always the occasional bully who will threaten you with a nuisance suit, threaten to do damage to your reputation, threaten to blacklist you with your clientele. He, too, is backed up by his "gang"—a few other business associates who don't like you and an attorney.

When some unjust thing like this happens you might do what we did when a principal we were working for as a Finder several years ago tried to cover over the completion of a transaction and cheat us out of our fee. We started out with the usual one to one ratio formula: threatening civil suit. Then geared up for the "hit-him-with-everything-but-the-kitchen-sink" plusses. Because the transaction was of a type that involved the "propriety" of the man's fee structure, a type that was at that time under investigation by the S.E.C., we sent a letter to this Government Agency, giving them a "case in point" to investigate. It so happened that the F.T.C. was piggy-backing on this kind of practice, too, so we also sent them a letter. Because promises involving flagrant falsehoods were involved in letters to us, we also sent photocopies to the Inspection Division of the United States Post Office, due to possible mail fraud. We also alerted by letter, the Better Business Bureau of his community, the State Attorney General's Office, and the Intelligence Division of the I.R.S. (because of suspected tax fraud). We knew that the man's operation was a borderline case, that he could probably defend himself. (He was no dummy.) Point is, we poured it on so heavily that the man never knew, from week-to-week, which flank he would have to defend next.

Can you imagine getting a letter threatening civil suit, with photocopies of all documents and the bottom reading:

cc: Securities & Exchange Commission
cc: Federal Trade Commission
cc: Inspection Division, U. S. Post Office Dept.
cc: Better Business Bureau
cc: State Attorney General's Office
cc: Internal Revenue Service, Intelligence Division

What would you think? In addition to being mad, confused, and with a slight jump in your blood pressure, you might think it best to settle before the avalanche smothers you.

This is what we call the ten to one ratio. And, when we reminded this gentleman that these various governmental investigative actions initiated by us *were only for "starters"* and that in the coming months at least ten more would be launched, guess what! We suddenly got paid.

This chapter covers the major pitfalls and pratfalls you'll run into in the Finders' business (every business has them). However, if you follow the general guidelines as laid down here, you should be able to keep these to a minimum.

CHAPTER 7

The Grand Slam—How to Make a Fortune in Finders' Fees

THIS IS THE LONGEST chapter in this book, for an excellent reason: *It presents to you a thorough blueprint for what we believe to be the greatest opportunity in the entire Finders' fee field.*

Options:

1. If you're an exceptionally brilliant, well-experienced, *all-around* businessman, you could just possibly do this yourself.
2. We mentioned earlier that a tie-in with a management consultant is one of the very best. In this chapter you'll see why, in it's precise form.
3. This possibility is *so big* that it could very easily go over the bounds of a relationship with a single management consultant. It might require you to establish a small firm, combining the additions of a marketing expert, a sharp accountant and a (staff) attorney.

The key to this is "The Integrated Marketing Audit." In the late 1950s we filled in something similar to the long questionnaire which will follow with executives of Chicken of the Sea, Minute Maid, Pillsbury Mills, Carnation Milk, Dole Hawaiian Pineapple, several other major food processors and many small companies in other manufacturing fields. About one hour's time is required for the gathering of a *complete marketing profile* of any company. It is so all-encompassing, so all-revealing, that once filled in, you'll instantly see five, ten, fifteen or more ways to make Finders' fees—*from a single company.*

One marketing executive, who looked bored in the beginning stages of answering these many questions, looked plaintively out of his top story executive suite office, upon completion of the last question, hesitated for nearly a half minute, breathed a deep sigh, and said, "You know, that thing *really* makes you think."

For that same reason, you, too, might become a bit bored while reading the beginning phases of this questionnaire. But as you read, note carefully the many reciprocal and "trap" questions. The company "size-up" possibilities will hit you. You'll note the pile-up of vital information about the company that is going into your head. And, mostly, note the opportunity after opportunity "situations" which will pop out at you from the words themselves, between the words, the lines themselves, between the lines, and the significance of every check mark made. At the conclusion of the presentation of this lengthy questionnaire, we'll review some of the many opportunities you'll see, to be of service to the company, and earn some astounding Finders' Fees for yourself.

For the sake of "overallism," we'll call the company the Garbled Goods Mfg. Co., manufacturers of both industrial and consumer products. Actually, a similar questionnaire can be devised to apply to *any kind of business known to man.*

THE INTEGRATED MARKETING AUDIT
(A Questionnaire)

Company ______________________________
Headquarters ______________________________
Address ______________________________
City & State ______________________________
Other plant(s) located in ______________________________
____
____
____

President ______________________________
Executive Vice President ______________________________
Vice President in charge of
Sales/Marketing ______________________________
Advertising Director ______________________________
Engineering Dept. Manager ______________________________
Other key Administrative
Executives ______________________________
____
____
____
____
____

PART I—ABOUT YOUR PRODUCTION . . .

How is your production divided?

Job-order (custom) manufacture ____ %

Repetitive (standard) manufacture ____ %

Total should equal 100%

What % of your total production is for:

Private label ____ %

Sold under your own name ____ %

Total should equal 100%

Do you sub-contract . . .

Liberally ( ) Moderately ( ) Lightly ( )?

%-wise, about how does this break down? ____________

What % of your production is for export? ____ %

What countries outside the U.S. and its possessions? ____________

(note: place a 1, 2 and 3 next to your biggest outside-the-U.S. markets.)

Figuring production capacity as 100%, at what *current* % of production capacity are you now operating? ____%. What additional % *could* you add, to capacity (100%), *in one year,* in order to accommodate additional sales? ____%. What is the minimum % of production at which you must operate (by currently figured operating ratios) in order to break even? ____ %

Is your production seasonal? Highly ( ) Moderately ( ) Practically no factor ( )

At which times during the year is it at its peak? Spring ( ) Summer ( ) Fall ( ) Winter ( )

Are your operations restricted by federal, state or local legislation? Closely restricted ( ) Moderately restricted ( ) Negligible factor ( )

If closely or moderately restricted, explain briefly

____

____

List just a few of your major suppliers

____

____

____

____

PART II—ABOUT YOUR MARKETS . . .

If you don't have the answers to the following readily at hand, your rough estimates will be good enough . . .

	Last year	*5 years ago*
Total industry sales	$ ______	$ ______
Your share of this	______ %	______ %
Competitors' *combined* share of this	______ %	______ %
Total should equal	100%	100%

Generally, what % of your *total* business volume is derived from . . .

Consumer Market	______ %
Industrial Market	______ %
Misc.: Trade, Professional, etc.	______ %
Total should equal	100%

Now, to break this down further—to markets within markets . . .

Very approximately, what product lines do you sell in your specific markets . . . through which channels of distribution . . . and, if you care to tell us, very roughly, what % of saturation (100%) do you feel you've achieved in these markets?

MARKET (Describe, or give S.I.C. numbers	PRODUCTS (list strongest selling items first)	CHANNEL OF DISTRIBUTION	% MARKET SATURATION
			%
			%
			%
			%
			%
			%
			%
			%
			%
			%
			%
			%
			%
			%
			%
			%
			%
			%

List your leading competitors (first, second, then third, closest to you in products similar to those you manufacture)

	Name	National Yes	National No	Strongest Markets	Strongest Products
1	________	( )	( )	________	________
2	________	( )	( )	________	________
3	________	( )	( )	________	________

(Under "strongest products," above, check those that are strong because of a *price* advantage over you)

How many *new* competitors have you taken on in the past three years? ______ Have any of these *new* competitors been racking up remarkable sales gains? Yes ( ) No ( )

If yes, who? ____________ In what product line? ____________

____________ ____________

PART III—ABOUT YOUR PRODUCTS . . .

Approximately, how many individual products do you manufacture (standardized)? ____________

What is the size (dollar) of your average sale (to your end-customer)? ____________

What is your product turnover ratio (how many times purchased within one year?) ____________

Approximately what % of your customers become "repeat" customers? _____%

What are your best products—from among the items in your line—from the standpoint of profitability per unit (highest margin items)? ____

____

____

Do you sell any "leader" items (items which carry little or no margin—items that are carried in the line merely to establish the important *first sale* to a new customer? Yes ( ) No ( ) If yes, what are these items? ____

____

We're sure you're aware that, in analyses of many companies' sales records, it is not uncommon to find that 15% of the items in a fairly long line account for 50% or more of total sales volume, while another 15% may bring in 2% or less. Have you ever made a *comprehensive* study to clearly differentiate between your "live" and "dead" products? Yes ( ) No ( ) If yes, what % *could* you drop without affecting your sales/profit picture appreciably? _____% What are these items? ____

____

____

____

PART IV—ABOUT YOUR MARKETING RESEARCH . . .

(Note: In the following questions we wish to determine, only, which categories are covered by an actual, formal research program. Please do *not* check the categories in which you rely primarily upon the mature, experienced judgments of yourself and your staff.)

Do you have an actual "Research Program" to determine the following? . . .

Actual and potential markets ( ) *Present* uses and applications of your products ( ) Prospect knowledge of your products ( ) Possible *new* uses and applications of your products ( ) Common misconceptions that may affect the sale of your products ( ) Buying motivations ( ) Buying practices within markets ( ) Service requirements ( ) Product volume by *types* of outlets ( ) General economic trends ( ) Marketability of new products ( ) Marketability of related products (slight revisions of products in your line) ( ) Effect on product procedures ( ) Capital requirements ( ) Best selling appeals ( ) Extent of competitive activity ( ) Attitudes of salesmen ( ) Attitudes of distributors ( ) Operating proficiency of salesmen ( ) Operating proficiency of distributors ( ) Best means for movement of products (Physical—warehousing, transportation, etc.) ( ) Packaging preferences ( ) Pricing policies ( ) Advertising and sales promotion results ( ) Potential sales ( )

What trade associations do you belong to? ____________________

____

____

How much do you use and rely upon the *market* research (not technical research) activities of such organizations? A great deal ( ) Moderately ( ) Very little ( )

If you have an advertising agency, does it provide research facilities? Complete ( ) Partial ( ) None ( )

Do you use these facilities?
Often ( ) Occasionally ( ) Never ( )

Which facets of your organization are *primarily* responsible for what research you *do* engage in? Market Research Dept. ( ) Sales Dept. ( ) Advertising Dept. ( ) A technical department (such as R & D, Engineering, Laboratory, New Product Development Dept., etc.) ( )

Which *outside* organizations assist you in the *integration and interpretation* of what research you do? None ( ) Advertising Agency ( ) Marketing Research Agency ( ) Marketing counsel ( ) Management counsel ( ) Other: ________

____

____

What do you believe to be the sales potential for your products? 2 years hence $______ 5 years $______ 10 years $______

PERTAINING TO YOUR *CONSUMER* MARKET PRODUCT *ONLY* . . .

Are your customers the general public ( ) . . . or, a *special classification* of the general public (e.g., women or men; certain age brackets; certain ethnic groups; certain income categories; certain occupations.

Please elaborate in a few words on which special *classification groups* you checked ______________________

____

____

____

Are your products more of the "impulse sale" type ( ) . . . or, the "planned purchase" type? ( )

In your market, which do you believe to be the most important factor? Price ( ) Quality ( ) Other: ______________________

____

Who are the *secondary* influences behind the purchase of your products? Husband ( ) Wife ( ) Children ( ) Doctor ( ) Dentist ( ) Educators ( ) Beautician ( ) Barber ( ) Lawyer ( ) Religious Leaders ( ) Mechanic ( ) Contractor ( ) Tradesmen ( ) Fraternal or social groups ( ) High income or influential people ( ) Other: ______________________

____

PERTAINING TO YOUR *INDUSTRIAL AND TRADE MARKET* PRODUCT *ONLY* . . .

Who are your *primary* buyers?

1. Title: ______________________________
2. Title: ______________________________
3. Title: ______________________________
4. Other titles: ______________________________

____

Who are the *secondary* influences behind the purchase of your products (list by job title again & in order of what you consider to be order of diminishing importance)?

1. ______________________________
2. ______________________________
3. ______________________________
4. ______________________________
5. ______________________________
6. ______________________________

In order to identify and grade these *levels* of influence, which *one* of the following four methods do you rely upon the most?

Long established knowledge and practice ( ) Research by media serving these markets ( ) Trade association information ( ) Specific research of your own (either by your own organization, or, with the help of outside research and counsel) ( )

PART V—ABOUT YOUR PRODUCT DEVELOPMENT . . .

How long has it been since you've engaged in *major* product redesign? Within past year ( ) 1-3 years ( ) 3-10 years ( ) 10 years or more ( )

Do you have at least *one* full-time Designer on your staff? Yes ( ) No ( ) Do you have any R & D activity at all? Yes ( ) No ( ) Is all such activity sub-contracted? Yes ( ) No ( ) If you sub-contract to an outside, independent firm, how often? Often ( ) Occasionally ( ) Never ( )

Check *three* only of the following—what you consider to be the *most* important reasons for redesigning products . . . Bolster sales ( ) Meet competition ( ) Meet needs for up-graded products ( ) Cut production costs ( ) To take advantage of lower-cost materials ( ) To reduce scrap and/or waste ( )

By whom are your packages designed?
Package Designer ( ) Advertising Agency ( )
Printer ( ) Within your own organization ( ) . . .
If so, by whom? ____________________
Other: ____________________
____
____

Very roughly, what are your average manufacturing costs and add-on selling prices?

Manufacturing cost $______
Price to Middlemen who sell to other Middlemen $______
Price to Middlemen who sell to end-customers $______
End selling price $______

Are your developmental costs in proper proportion to your manufacturing costs?
Yes ( ) No ( )

If you have another or unusual method of selling-price add-ons (e.g., consignment), please explain briefly: ______________________

____

Which *one* of the following three considerations do you feel is the *most* important consideration in pricing products?

Adequate to protect profit margin ( ) Price competitively—in line with current "going" prices for comparable products ( ) Priced at best level at which product can be introduced quickly to influential segment of market ( )
Other: ______________________________________

____

What's your warranty policy (if any)? ______________________
What's your installation policy (if any)? ______________________
What's your service policy (if any)? ______________________

Do you "pre-test" your new products (market them in limited markets) before placing them on the general market for sale?
Always ( ) Often ( ) Occasionally ( ) Never ( )

PART VI—ABOUT YOUR SALES AND DISTRIBUTION . . .

(Note—In this section we ask many questions concerning the physical make-up of your sales and distribution structure. *If* your sales and distribution is extremely diversified, apply your answers here to your *leading* markets *only*. We wish to keep the "Pattern" of your response as simple and clear [to us] as possible.)

How much of your line is . . .

Manufactured *by* you	______%
Manufactured *for* you (under your private label)	______%
Total should equal	100%

Is your distribution . . . National ( ) Regional ( )

If regional, in what areas? ________________________________

____

If national, what are your *strongest* areas? ________________

____

Check the brackets that best describe the subdivision lines of your sales organization

Territorial subdivisions ( ) Subdivision by *type* of customer ( ) Subdivision by *type* of product ( ) Other:

____

Do you maintain "house" accounts (accounts on which no sales commissions are paid)?

Yes ( ) No ( )

How many salesmen do you have?______ Of these, how many are "missionary" salesmen (salesmen who open accounts for your distributors)?______ How many are allowed to carry other lines?______

Do you use . . . Your own ( ) . . . Leased ( ) . . . or Public ( ) warehousing facilities? How many warehouses do you have goods in?______ What is your ratio of warehousing costs to total sales costs?______ Are your warehouse layouts standardized? Yes ( ) No ( ) If no, explain: ____________________

What basic compensation system do you use? (For your salesmen.)

Straight salary ( ) Salary & commission ( ) Straight commission ( )

If commission is involved, do you maintain a "draw" against commission? Yes ( ) No ( )

Who writes your Catalogs (if any)?

Sales Dept. ( ) Advertising Dept. ( ) Engineering Dept. ( ) Advertising Agency ( ) Free-lance writer ( ) Combination ( ) If so, what combination?

____

____

Other: ______________________________

____

What selling *equipment* do you make available to your salesmen and distributors?

(Note: Encircle the S after the pieces furnished *your own* salesmen . . . Encircle D after the pieces furnished your distributors' salesmen)

Easel Display S D Sample Case S D Loose Leaf Display Folder S D Sales Literature S D Sales Manual S D Service Manual S D Order Forms S D Product Samples S D Sales Report Forms S D Stationery S D "Records" material (e.g., prospect, customer record books, files, other) S D Complete Presentation Kits involving a variety of materials S D Other: S__________________ D__________________

__________________ __________________

Do you maintain a formal sales training program? For Salesmen ( ) . . . For Distributors ( ) If you do, how long are these training periods? For Salesmen ____________________________

For Distributors ____________________________

Naturally, due to the limitations of practicality, and the time and expense element, you place *greater* emphasis on some phases of your sales training program (if you have one) than you do on others. Please check the following categories by "degree" of emphasis. (Note: Place an S in the brackets that apply to your *own* Salesmen, and a D in the brackets that apply to your Distributors'.)

	Lightly	*Moder-ately*	*Heavily*
Company orientation—history, organization and physical make-up	( )	( )	( )
Theoretical training in selling techniques	( )	( )	( )
Market orientation	( )	( )	( )
Product orientation	( )	( )	( )
Policies on credit, services, adjustments, prices and delivery	( )	( )	( )
Obligations to company	( )	( )	( )
Systematizing—time control and work organization	( )	( )	( )
Servicing customers	( )	( )	( )
Sales follow-up	( )	( )	( )
Sales equipment (how to use)	( )	( )	( )
Sales territories	( )	( )	( )
Advertising & Sales promotion (familiarization)	( )	( )	( )
Merchandising procedures	( )	( )	( )
Other: ______________________	( )	( )	( )
Other: ______________________	( )	( )	( )
Other: ______________________	( )	( )	( )

How often do you hold sales meetings, clinics or conferences? (Note: Place an N in the brackets that indicate national clinics . . . place an R in the brackets that indicate regional meetings.)

	No set time	*Weekly*	*Monthly*	*Quarterly*	*Twice yearly*	*Annually*
Your own Salesmen:	( )	( )	( )	( )	( )	( )
Distributors':						
______________	( )	( )	( )	( )	( )	( )
______________	( )	( )	( )	( )	( )	( )
______________	( )	( )	( )	( )	( )	( )

How many branch sales offices do you maintain?_____ Are your regional sales meetings conducted . . . at these branch offices ( ) . . . on your Distributors' premises ( ) . . . or, through privately arranged facilities (hotels' meeting rooms, etc.)? ( ) How many middlemen do you do business with, and what % of your product is sold through these various middlemen (first give *number* of outlets, then % of total output that moves through these channels . . . for example, you may deal with 230 brokers, whose commissions are attached to 65% of your output, and, say 1,100 jobbers are involved with another 15% of your output, etc.)?

COMMISSION MIDDLEMEN: Brokers _____% Dealers _____%
Manufacturers' Representatives _____% Other: _____%

MIDDLEMEN WHO TAKE TITLE TO GOODS: Jobbers _____%
Dealers _____% Discount & Mail Order Houses _____%
Wholesalers _____% Central Buying Groups _____% Industrial Distributors _____% Retailers _____% Other: _____%

DIRECT TO CUSTOMER: Direct Salesmen _____% Outlet Stores _____% Club Plan _____% Direct Mail Order _____% Other: _____%

If you have an *unusual* method of distribution, please describe (briefly) here ____

____

____

Do you have a set *formula* for selecting distributors ( ) . . . or, do you rely chiefly on the experienced judgment of people within your own organization ( )

Check *two* only of the following four points—the two points you consider to be the *most* important points to look for when selecting a distributor . . .

Solvency ( ) Aggressive Reputation ( ) Ease of Working Relationship ( ) Volume of Business ( ) Revolutionary Ideas ( )

What types of sales incentives do you offer (either regularly or periodically) to your sales-distributor organiaztion? (Note: Encircle S for incentives that apply to your *own* Salesmen . . . encircle D for incentives that apply to your *distributors'*.)

Merchandise S D Cash S D Honor awards S D
Travel S D Other: S D ____________________________

____

Does your distribution "pattern" vary—by region? Varies by region ( ) Fundamentally uniform ( ) . . . *if* your distribution "pattern" varies by region, why? Shipping advantages ( ) To get closer to markets ( ) Inadequate warehousing ( ) Other: ______________________

Which *best* describes your territorial policy? Exclusive to own salesmen ( ) Exclusive, but with split accounts ( ) Substantially overlap ( )

Are your sales territories roughly equivalent (geographically) to those of your leading competitors? Yes ( ) No ( )

What *base* do you use, *primarily,* for setting up your sales quotas? Salesmen and/or Distributor estimates ( ) U.S. Government figures ( ) Sales Forecasting process (evolved through your own market research) ( ) Other: ______________
____

What are your trade discounts? ______________________
____
____

Check the terms of sale you employ . . .

Mandatory pre-payment ( )
C. O. D. ( )
Consignment ( )
Refund guarantee for unsold merchandise ( )
Open account ( )
Special franchise agreements ( )
Quantity discounts ( )
Conditional sales contracts ( )
Chattel Mortgage ( )
f.o.b. factory ( )
f.o.b. destination ( )
Any special arrangement for sharing freight charges ( )

Other: ______

Do you grant any "special" deals (to stimulate trade)?
Often ( ) Occasionally ( ) Never ( )

What types of special concessions do you grant? Early deliveries ( )
Freight absorption ( ) Rebates ( ) Reciprocal sales ( )
"Special" prices (off-list) ( ) Easy, long-term open account credit ( ) Other: ______

Do you drop-ship? Often ( ) Occasionally ( ) Never ( )

What is your returned goods percentage? ____%

What is your bad debt (uncollected accounts) percentage? ____%

Which *one* of the following three *best* describes your policy governing returns and refusals?

Unconditional Guarantee—immediate refund for any reason ( )

Limited Guarantee—refund for clear-cut failure of quality, late delivery, poor packing, etc. ( )

No Guarantee—each case negotiated individually, as it arises ( )

In what *physical* form do you keep your sales records?

Card Files ( ) Letter Files ( ) Kardex ( ) Ledgers ( ) Roll-type ( ) Modified IBM, or IBM-type equipment ( ) Fully computerized ( )

Other: ____________________

How often do your salesmen send in reports?

Daily ( ) Weekly ( ) Semi-Monthly ( ) Bi-Monthly ( ) Quarterly ( )

Other: ____________________

What is your ratio of *sales to calls?* _____ sale out of every _____ calls

Basically, how is your salesmen's work organized?

Largely left to salesmen ( ) Company provides "routing" forms, suggestions, inquiries from advertising and other "helps" ( ) Salesmen's calls closely directed and tightly controlled by company ( )

What portion of your salesmen's time is spent on . . .

Actual calls on customers	____%
Actual calls on prospects	____%
Planning and preparation	____%
Travel	____%
Total should equal	100%

What is the *average* gross business done—per salesman—per year? $_____ What's the lowest? $_____ What's the highest? $_____

What is the *average* amount—*per salesman*—per year—spent on sales "back-up" (sum total of all sales promotion, advertising, public relations expenditures, etc., divided by the number of salesmen)? $ ________

What is the *average* of *all other* costs incurred—*per salesman*—per year (e.g., recruiting, training, administrative costs, out-of-pocket expenses, salesman's expense accounts, etc.) ? $ ________

PERTAINING TO YOUR *CONSUMER* MARKET PRODUCTS ONLY . . .

If you sell through retail outlets, check types . . .
Automotive Parts Stores ( ) Drug Stores ( ) Supermarkets ( ) Other types of Grocery or "Specialty" Food Stores ( ) Caterers ( ) Discount Houses ( ) Appliance Stores ( ) Wagon Routes ( ) Variety Stores ( ) Gift and Stationery Shops ( ) Department Stores ( ) Paint and Hardware Stores ( ) Clothing Stores ( ) Gas Stations and Car Garages ( ) Restaurants and other away-from-home Eating Establishments ( ) Furniture Stores ( ) Garden Supply Stores ( ) Building Supply Stores ( ) Photo Shops ( ) Confectionery Stores ( ) Jewelry Stores ( ) Barber or Beauty Shops ( ) Shoe Stores ( ) Laundries ( ) Cleaning Establishments ( ) Other: ________________________

____

____

Do you try to standardize your prices closely to the market? Strictly ( ) On some products ( ) None ( ) Price by what we think market will bear ( ) Try to undercut competition by slight margin ( ) Try to undercut competition by wide margin, shoot for bigger profits on far bigger volume ( )

List your *top three* retail outlets, by type . . .

Outlet	*Number of Stores Handling Your Line*	*% of your total volume*
____________	____________	____________ %
____________	____________	____________ %
Misc.: All other outlets combined	____________	____________ %
Total should equal		100%

List your *bottom three* retail outlets, by type . . .

Outlet	*Number of Stores Handling Your Line*	*% of your total volume*
____________	____________	____________ %
____________	____________	____________ %
____________	____________	____________ %

What merchandising techniques are generally used by these outlets? Demonstration ( ) Extensive window and interior displays ( ) Mail order selling ( ) Handbills ( ) Local newspaper publicity ( ) Local newspaper advertising ( ) Use of advertising specialties ( ) Liberal credit ( ) Multiple unit selling ( ) Related product selling ( ) Store-wide sales ( ) Premiums ( )

Contests ( ) Limited-time free trials ( ) Radio advertising ( ) Ticket agency facilities ( ) Television advertising ( ) Telephone directory advertising ( ) Outdoor advertising ( ) Truck panel advertising ( ) Car card advertising ( ) Billboard advertising ( ) Public relations (sponsorship of luncheons, banquets, fashion shows, autographing parties for celebrities, etc.) ( )

Other: ____________________

What "operations" aids and merchandising help do *you* provide these outlets and what % (of total *number* of outlets) are *using* these aids?

Cost control systems ( ) _____% Store layout plans and advice ( ) _____% Promotion calendars ( ) _____% Visual aids ( ) _____% Fixtures ( ) _____% Financial assistance ( ) _____% Inventory control systems ( ) _____% Bookkeeping systems ( ) _____% Personal, in-store promotional help ( ) _____% Traffic building suggestions and studies ( ) _____% Mat services ( ) _____% Cooperative advertising/promotion allowances ( ) _____% Aisle units ( ) _____% Racks ( ) _____% Dispensers ( ) _____% Advertising clocks or other turning, attention-getting gimmicks ( ) _____% General display materials ( ) _____% Decals ( ) _____% Containers ( ) _____% Dealer identification signs ( ) _____% Wrapping materials ( ) _____% Radio and/or TV scripts ( ) _____% Package stuffers ( ) _____% Other: ____________________

____

____________________ _____%

PART VII—ABOUT YOUR COMMUNICATIONS . . .

INTERNAL COMMUNICATIONS:

What media do you use for consolidating all facets of your own sales organization?

Personal consultations ( ) Direct mail (sales letters, bulletins, broadsides, flyers, etc.) ( ) Internal house organ ( ) Bulletin board ( ) Other: ____________
____

TRADE RELATIONS:

What media do you use for consolidating all facets of your distributor organization?

	Commission Middle*men (e.g., Brokers, Manufacturers' Reps)*	*Middlemen who take title to goods (e.g., Wholesalers)*	*Direct Salesmen to Consumer*
Personal consultations (including sales meetings, etc.)	( )	( )	( )
Selling aids—to help sell (as enumerated under SALES & DISTRIBUTION)	( )	( )	( )
Direct Mail	( )	( )	( )
House Organs	( )	( )	( )
Films	( )	( )	( )
Cassettes	( )	( )	( )
Trade magazine advertising	( )	( )	( )
Trade magazine publicity	( )	( )	( )
Trade show exhibits	( )	( )	( )
Advertising specialties	( )	( )	( )
Closed circuit TV	( )	( )	( )
Gifts	( )	( )	( )
Other: ______________________	( )	( )	( )

Do you provide samples?

Abundantly ( ) Some ( ) None ( )

ABOUT YOUR GENERAL MARKET DEVELOPMENT . . .

What media do you use to reach your *end-customers* and prospective *end-customers* . . .

Point of purchase material ( ) Direct mail ( ) Consumer magazine advertising ( ) Consumer magazine publicity ( ) Trade magazine advertising (if a trade is your end-customer) ( ) Newspaper advertising ( ) Newspaper publicity ( ) Radio advertising ( ) Radio publicity ( ) Television advertising ( ) Television publicity ( ) Outdoor advertising ( ) Films ( ) Premiums ( ) Package inserts ( ) Other: ____________________

____

ABOUT YOUR PUBLIC RELATIONS . . .

Do you engage in a general "goodwill-building" program (embracing all the major techniques of public relations to gain increased recognition and consolidation of your standing in your own community, in your own industry, among customers and prospects, the government, your own employees, stockholders, etc.)?

Never have ( ) Did in the past, but not currently ( ) Am *currently* engaged in ( ) Intend to in the future ( ) Do *not* intend to in the future ( ) Undecided ( )

Do you have a publicity department? Yes ( ) No ( )

Do you use advertising agency publicity services?
Yes ( ) No ( )

Do you have a company "news service" for transmittal of *all* types of news of your company to the following media . . .
Local newspapers ( ) Consumer magazines ( ) Wire services ( ) Trade magazines ( ) Radio stations ( ) Television stations ( ) Directory and reference materials publishers ( ) Other: ______________
____

Do you use Public Relations *advertising* (strictly institutional type) in . . .
Trade magazines ( ) Consumer magazines ( ) Newspapers ( ) Radio ( ) Television ( ) Transportation media ( ) Other: ______________
____

PART VIII—ABOUT YOUR OUTSIDE CONTACTS . . .

(In everyday business, constant personal contacts are necessary, not only with the customers and prospects, but with purveyors of goods and services that enable the manufacturer to *better* sell and service his customers and prospects. Learning the *extent* to which you use the many various outside organizations available to you is, thus, vitally important to this project.)

Do you have an advertising agency? Yes ( ) No ( )

If yes, who? ______________________

St. Address ______________________

City & State ______________ Zip Code ________

Phone ______________________

Is your relationship: Exceptionally close ( ) Average ( ) They handle the "Mechanics" only (e.g., preparation and placement of ads, direct mail, etc.) ( ) Who is the Account Executive on your account? ______________________

What liaison do you maintain with the following organizations? (Note: Where both you *and* your advertising agency handle contact, check multiple columns.)

	Close & we handle	*Adv. Ag'cy handles*	*No appreciable contact*
Management consultant	( )	( )	( )
Marketing Research agencies	( )	( )	( )
Public Relations agencies	( )	( )	( )
Mailing list brokers and compilers	( )	( )	( )
Sales Promotion & Merchandising agencies	( )	( )	( )
Other service cos. (e.g., clipping bureaus)	( )	( )	( )
Trade associations (mfgrs. of similar products)	( )	( )	( )
Trade associations (customers & prospects)	( )	( )	( )
Trade associations (advertising & sales)	( )	( )	( )
Government agencies	( )	( )	( )
Media (all types)	( )	( )	( )
Suppliers (tangible—printers, display cos., etc.)	( )	( )	( )
Professional Finders	( )	( )	( )

(*Author's note: Playing it "by ear," you could point out that you work as a Finder, too—in addition to consulting services, if you must . . . for most frequently you will get the "No appreciable contact" check-off as an answer to this question. But, at this late stage in the interview, the company representative who is cooperating in the questionnaire quiz cannot be anything but impressed with your "in-depth" probing into the cogent and vital affairs of his business structure. If you were to point out that you can see many areas where you can help, on a contingent fee basis—no results, no fee—you could catch his interest before finishing the interview . . . your first essential big step toward later making specific Finders' fee arrangements for a variety of searches.*)

	Close & we handle	*Adv. Ag'cy handles*	*No appreciable contact*
Other: ________________	( )	( )	( )
Other: ________________	( )	( )	( )
Other: ________________	( )	( )	( )

What trade papers do you read? ________________

________________ ________________

________________ ________________

________________ ________________

PART IX—ABOUT YOUR MANAGEMENT OPERATING TECHNIQUES AND BUDGETS . . .

Do you subscribe to the relatively new theory of "integrated marketing management?" Yes ( ) No ( ) Undecided ( )
If yes, do you relate this theory to practice? Currently set up, functionally, along this line ( ) Haven't yet, but definitely intend to ( )

(Note: In the following four questions: we mean by *primarily*, who carries *the most* responsibility—in reporting to top management on the various stages of programming. Where equal responsibility exists, check more than one classification.)

Who is *primarily* responsible for *planning* sales/advertising programs —in the embryonic stage (interpreting market research, getting ideas together, sales approaches, themes, etc., integrated and "off the ground," so to speak)?
Sales Dept. ( ) Advertising Dept. ( ) Market Research Dept. ( ) Top Management ( ) Advertising Agency ( ) Marketing Counsel ( )
Other: ____________________

Who is then *primarily* responsible for *developing* coordinated sales/advertising strategy from that point to finished program?
Sales Dept. ( ) Advertising Dept. ( ) Market Research Dept. ( ) Advertising Agency ( ) Marketing or Management Counsel ( ) Other: ____________

Who affixes final recommendation for campaigns and programs when they are submitted to top management for formal "go ahead" approval?

Sales Vice President ( ) Marketing Vice President ( ) Executive Vice President ( ) Administrative Assistant ( ) Market Research Dept. ( ) Advertising Agency ( ) Marketing or Management Counsel ( )
Other: ______________________________

Who is *primarily* responsible for *administering* the program *after* it is put into operation?

Sales Promotion Dept. ( ) Sales Dept. ( ) Marketing Dept. ( ) Advertising Dept. ( )
Other: ______________________________

Very roughly: how are your marketing costs (overall) allocated?

Sales Administration (including distribution, market research costs, etc.)	_____%
Advertising Administration (including appropriations for both measured & unmeasured media)	_____%
Trade & Public Relations	_____%
Total should equal	100%

Of the following listed methods, check those that best describe the approach you take in making up your advertising budget . . .

- % of past sales ( )
- % of anticipated sales ( )
- Task system (requirements for job to be done ( )
- Underlying financial strength of the co. (capability) ( )
- Arbitrary sum ( )

What % of your total advertising budget goes into these media categories?

- National consumer advertising _____%
- Local consumer advertising _____%
- Cooperative advertising (with others) _____%
- Misc.: (e.g., contributions to trade association campaigns, etc.) _____%

Total should equal 100 %

What % of your *total* advertising goes into your top three markets?

1. ________________ _____%
2. ________________ _____%
3. ________________ _____%

Misc.: all other markets combined _____%

Total should equal 100%

If marketing *consumer* products, how does your advertising budget break down (percentage-wise, in these major media)?

- Radio-Television _____%
- Transportation-Outdoor _____%
- Misc. and unmeasured media (e.g., direct mail, etc.) _____%

Total should equal 100%

On *average,* how many new prospect sales "leads"—through your advertising—are you able to send out per month?

To your own salesmen ______ To middlemen selling to other middlemen ______ To middlemen selling your end-customers ______

Does your Sales Dept. generally follow up on its inquiries received through your advertising?

Always ( ) Occasionally ( ) Never ( )

Do you have set formulas for screening, evaluating and processing inquiries . . . or, do you rely primarily upon your own experienced judgment (or that of someone else within your organization) for determining who are prospects and who are not?

Use set formula ( ) Use own judgment( )

PART X—CHECKLIST

We can gain *much ammunition,* to upgrade this project, from many of the *routine* forms and printed material that you can provide—material that you use in the everyday operation of your business. So that we can do a *better* job in our quest of providing "directional guidance" that will afford increased, and more profitable, sales—for *you*—we would like to have samples of the following forms (blank copies) and printed pieces (the items you *do* have, of course). Please check off, below, the specific pieces you are supplying with this questionnaire. This material will serve us well, both while we are working on our proposed program for you, and, as an "inventory checklist" in case you would like this material returned at the conclusion of this project. *Any* of the following materials will be helpful:

Samples of labels of a cross section of your products	( )	Salesmen's indoctrination book	( )
Price Lists	( )	Sample Service Manual pages	( )
Parts Lists	( )	Salesmen's Report Forms	( )
"Sales Agreement" contract forms (salesmen's contracts, franchise agreement forms, etc.)	( )	Salesmen's Expense Report Form	( )
Samples of all public relations materials	( )	Routing and/or call scheduling forms	( )
		Financial Statement (if made public)	( )

Field Summary Sheets (used in Sales control) ( )
Sales Work Sheets ( )
Order Forms ( )
Samples of customer record forms ( )
Samples of prospect record forms ( )
Samples of suppliers' bid forms ( )
Tear sheets of a variety of ads ( )

Photo or reproduction of recent trade show exhibit ( )
Organization chart—marketing function ( )
Organization chart—overall co. ( )
Any work-flow charts you may have for sales, advertising, market research, or marketing depts. ( )

If you can think of any other materials that may be helpful, in addition to the items checked above, please list here ______________

____

____

____

What other significant points can you add . . . points that will enable us to do a *more complete* job for you (e.g., relative failure or success of various campaigns; any experienced observations, special considerations, etc., that do not lend themselves to the "classification system" employed in this Questionnaire. And, *most important,* what about your objectives? How far do you desire to go? How are you thinking of getting there? How long do you think it should take? What sales goals do you hope to achieve, and approximately how much are you willing to invest to achieve them?) All the over-and-above information you care to include will be helpful.

____

____

____

____

____

____

____

____

____

____

____

____

____

(Attach additional sheets, if more space is needed)

Signature __________________________

Title __________________________

Co. __________________________

St. Address __________________________

City & State ______________ Zip Code ______

Date Questionnaire
filled in ______________

IN LIKE FLYNN

This expression was common in the early 1940s, in depicting the presumably effective amorous exploits of the late movie actor, Errol Flynn. From a far different viewpoint, a *business* one, you don't have to be a brilliant Businessman to see that access to such a complete profile of a company's thinking, as reflected from its marketing and sales side, *can be turned into nothing but solid gold bullion for you.*

1. It is of immeasurable value to the consultant—purely from the consultant's side—in being able to help the company.
2. It is of immeasurable value to you as a Finder (we still prefer the title "Business Consultant" all the way around—in your case it can be one who "finds").

In our past experiences in filling in these Questionnaires for many companies, large and small, here are some of the benefits we were able to gain:

One small company impressed us so greatly with its complete self-discipline, aggressiveness, and its "on-top-of-everything" answers that we invested in its stock, and in one year made a tidy profit.

One company whose export was nil, yet had a small, lightweight product, ideal for export, we introduced to the proper export house and collected a Finder's fee.

Determining that the turnover ratio was too slow in a product that involved a minimum of dollar investment in re-tooling for an additional component to it, we convinced the company to do just this. We introduced the company to the "right" industrial designer who has since done business with them—going on fifteen years now. (We collected no fee on this one; it was a favor to a friend.)

We were able to convince a company to drop from its line a "leader" item that was not doing its job—that is, it proved to be a one-time item which did not bring customers back for more of the company's products; sales stopped right there. We found a finder for the company, who in turn dug up an ideal new "leader" item for them that made sales literally flow right into the higher-profit items in the company's line.

We were able to convince a company treasurer that a certain portion of his company's line was wobbly because production was financed in the wrong way. Because there were frequent changes in design and tooling, we talked him out of a weird form of long-term financing the company engaged in, and into short-term lines of bank credit. It worked. The company was then able to "turn over" its financing about as fast as it turned over its design and tooling costs.

We suggested *films* for the sales meetings of one company whose products lent themselves to graphic display in gorgeous moving color. The company had never engaged in this kind of promotion. We introduced it to a small, but excellent producer of quality technicolor films, and a beautiful new business marriage was begun, one which lasted many years, till the company grew too big for a "small time" film producer, and engaged a larger one. (We took no fee on this one either; again, it was a favor to a friend.)

To a food company which encased a product which should have carried the connotation of maiden-like purity, we suggested they change the sickly green color of their package to an ivory white. We found for the company an ace package designer, who performed various services for them for many years afterward. (Yes, we did take a small fee on this one.)

We then got out of the consulting/finding field altogether, and plunged full-time into the publishing field—and when we started *BUSINESS OPPORTUNITIES DIGEST* in 1963 we made certain that we always published *plenty of specific Finders' fee offerings*—toward the (ah hem! noble and charitable) objective of making the wealthy *still wealthier.*

WHY NOT YOU TOO?

Now . . . let's go back over the Integrated Marketing Audit, for the moment, and see what you, *as a Finder* (whether you call yourself one or not) can do.

1. Check the export angle. Act as we did.
2. Check the sub-contract angle. Is it out of line? Could small-run pieces that the company is now manufacturing itself be done much more effectively and at lower cost by a sub-contractor? Find one.
3. Conversely, is the company operating at a *low* rate of capacity? Check its facilities. Turn the sub-contract thing around. Find another manufacturer who could use these facilities because he's overloaded. Collect a fee.
4. Is the company's line highly seasonable? Find an exporter who can equalize this handicap with a different climate. Collect a fee.
5. After finding out that, say 50% of a product line only brings in 5% or less of total sales, find a closeout or surplus buyer, 'cause the company is probably stuck with a big inventory. Collect a fee.
6. You'd be surprised how many companies—for some reason known only to God—use a *technical* department executive to do their *market* research. Find a competent outside contractor for them, knowledgeable in their field. Collect a fee.
7. Another major surprise is the number of companies which will answer "three to ten years" or even "ten years or more" when asked the question, "How long has it been since you've engaged

in major product redesign?" Such firms are ripe for new inventions. (Usually, when cross-checking against their new product development activity—or, rather inactivity—you'll find such companies are weak in all engineering areas. These are ripe for new inventions. Check the records of the U. S. Patent Office, study the classifieds of major magazines and newspapers and specialized magazines and newsletters. Find inventions that fit the company's line. And again, get paid for your efforts.

8. When you get the answer, "To take advantage of lower-cost materials," to the question, "What do you consider to be the *most* important reasons for redesigning products?" you can have a ball. Many small, and even tiny, manufacturers and suppliers are "red meat" prospects to approach for a Finders' fee deal if you can deliver big-quantity component orders. Bring them together with the firm that thinks in this way.

9. Surprise after surprise! You'll also discover that many companies will rely on a *printer* for their package design. Or, if done internally, this important function will be left to the hands of the drafting department or some other *technical* department. Depending upon the complexity, a package designer, graphic arts house, ad agency, sales promotion agency, or free-lancer operating in this field would be more appropriate.

10. When you hit the manufacturer who has a high percentage of products manufactured *for* him, under his private label, you've hit the jackpot. You can go literally berserk in the import field, new products, inventions, even surplus and closeout suppliers. Match up with his line. Collect fee after fee after fee.

11. The company which places *great* emphasis on company orientation, theoretical training in selling techniques, credit and price policies, and obligations to the company are among the mighty and the proud, those with a bit of a snobbish outlook and complacent attitude about their "position" in their market. You'll often find that this type of company will place a relatively light value on *sales equipment*—the bread and butter stuff the poor salesman must forge his living with. Suppliers in this field are too numerous to mention. Here, too, you can have a field

day working out deals with such suppliers. Each closed deal for a small fee, of course.

12. Most manufacturers want to "dump"—they want to manufacture their products, *sell* them to a middleman, get their money quickly and plow-back. There is a great opportunity for the financing Finder in this thinking pattern . . . for all too often it is more to the company's marketing advantage to deal through commission middlemen, or directly to the consumer. (You never hear of Avon or Fuller Brush bleeding, financially, do you?) Get the financing structure of the company turned into a *long-term* one that will allow for the slower flow of funds back into the corporate treasury, and collect a fee for the rearrangement.

13. Don't be flabbergasted if you get the answer, "Rely chiefly on the experienced judgment of people within our own organization," when asked how they go about selecting distributors. Dig further on this question and you'll frequently find that the Engineering Manager knows Joe Blow, who's got great coverage for them west of the Mississippi, the Inventory Control Manager knows the best Manufacturer's Rep in the South, and you got your Eastern and Middlewest covered by the biggest dealer in garbled goods through their Purchasing Agent who knows a Trade Association Executive who knows a retired Executive of Westinghouse who set it up through a guy who once worked for the U. S. Department of Commerce. Let your imagination run wild in such cases. You can make a Finder's fee deal with *each* of *many* distributors dying to get the Garbled Goods Mfg. Co.'s business.

14. When you get the answer, "Substantially overlap," you should be able to run the 100 in 8.9 too. This means simply that the company will sell to *anybody* who will buy—middlemen, consignment, free-lance agents, directly to retail outlets, for export, anywhere, anytime. With a company like this—if the line's a good one, of course—become it's sales agent. *Earn your fees that way.* And, your jaw will drop at how many manufacturing companies in the United States sell this way. Most will try to disguise this by answering, "Exclusive, but with "split

commission," because they're ashamed that their sales policies are so sloppy that they are really not in a position to protect anybody's commissions. But, you'll be able to see through it.

15. With the firm that grants "special deals" all over the place to stimulate sales you have your cue to make nearly any kind of a "special deal" for yourself too. Do it. And, collect a fee for each one.

16. When the returned goods percentage is abnormally high you've got sales possibilities to surplus houses—seconds and imperfects. *Cash-in!*

17. In analyzing what operational aids are supplied for retail outlet merchandising you can just about always find an example of the square peg in the round hole. Refer back to our recounting of the introduction of the company to the film producer, and you'll see what we mean. Find the square peg for the square hole, and the round peg for the round one, and you should be rewarded handsomely.

18. Part VIII—ABOUT YOUR OUTSIDE CONTACTS—is perhaps of the most vital importance to you, regarding the fattening of your wallet. In *every* case where the answer "No appreciable contact" is given, you could hardly miss. Even in many cases where the answer is "Advertising Agency handles," you have just about the same opportunity. In nineteen cases out of every twenty the company *thinks* its agency is handling it well, but they are actually doing a 1/10th job, or worse. Make the proper introductions, *collect the fees.*

19. When you learn that the man *primarily* responsible for *planning* the entire sales-advertising program is *also* the same man charged with the responsibility of *administering* it *after* it's put into operation, you've struck a rich vein of solid gold nuggets. He is a *key* man in the company. His judgment is relied upon heavily by all of his associates and subordinates. He is sharp, sharp, sharp. And, by nature, his intelligence, understanding, interest and overall business acumen make him the kind of person who will listen to *anything* that he can logically foresee as making more money and more profits for the com-

pany. Here you have an "ear." Don't muff the ball.

20. When an "arbitrary sum" is the answer you receive to "Check those (methods) that best describe the approach you take in making up your advertising budget," you are dealing with a ship without a captain. Be the consultant (if on your own); get your consultant into the act (if you're working with one) . . . or, go out and find the proper consultant, *and earn a Finder's fee.*

21. Generally speaking, the "set formula/own judgment" answers tell you priceless information about the company. When—and it all too often happens—"own judgment" is over-accented, you have the groundwork laid for approaches to fee deals of all sorts. Naturally, a careful "in-depth" assessment of the personality involved is a "must" here, for you'll often be dealing with a knuckle head who couldn't read a work-flow chart, even if his life depended on it. Psychology must predominate.

THERE'S GOLD TO BE MINED IN THEM THAR HILLS—WHAT ARE YOU WAITING FOR?

We've given you twenty-one concrete examples of overpowering and plentiful Finder's fee possibilities, drawn from the completed Integrated Marketing Audit of a *manufacturing company.* And there are loads more in that field alone. But, there's no reason whatever why *similar* forms cannot be made up *to cover all the other lush fields of finding.* Make one up for commodities and minerals dealers, stone wholesalers and importers, importers of all other kinds, exporters too, the "new products" boys, surplus and closeout merchants, antique dealers, real estate men, mortgage brokers, consultants, merger and acquisition specialists, other merchants, distributors, dealers and middlemen of all kinds. *The whole world is your market.*

In this field, your own head is your Board of Directors; a 10 x 10 room can house all of your necessities; your public library is your market research department; your fundamental graspings of rudimentary psychology opens your doors; and your positive, aggressive, straight-forward, and *fair-play* character and personality closes your sales . . . *and earns you your fees.*

CHAPTER 8

Consultant/Finder Case Histories

OVER THE YEARS that we have been out of the Finder's business, personally, we have granted permission to friends in the consulting field (more than 20% of the entire readership of *BUSINESS OPPORTUNITIES DIGEST* is made up of Business Consultants of one form or another) to adapt for their own use our Integrated Marketing Audit form.

Many of these people have used it "as is," others revised variations of the questionnaire to their own fields of interest. Some of their subsequent experiences—with and without use of the Audit—were fascinating, worth capsulizing for your how-to-do-it, how-not-to-do-it knowledge.

MANAGEMENT CONSULTING FROM A GARAGE

Quite a few years ago, George F., after some fifteen years of toil as a middle-management foundry executive, got fed up with the corporate rat race, remodeled his garage, converted it into an office, and set himself up as a Foundry Consultant.

George was no fool. He lived in a far-out suburb, a town of some 5,000 population, about forty miles from a large Eastern industrial city loaded with foundries.

He had a market. And, he figured he could do his business with these various firms out of a brief case on frequent trips to the big city, just as he'd done for fifteen years as a daily, long distance commuter to his job. He thus reasoned that none of his potential clients would be likely to visit him at his far-off office.

His own experience turned up a fact known to him previously, now confirmed by his audits of several other foundries: that a certain type sand (yes, sand) was far overpriced, and long distance freight made the price extra burdonsome. This particular type sand was considered indispensable to his only two clients who produced a specific type mould in big quantities which required it. In his new role, dealing with many foundries rather than one (servicing two, trying to "get in the door" with several others), he got into an idle conversation with a gabby salesman in a reception room one day. The man confided the fact that this sand variety was plentiful *and free* at a location just two hundred miles away. It was considered residue by a mining company which only wanted to get rid of it.

"These clowns!," George related to us the salesman's approximate words in mimicking his utter disdain for the purchasing agents he had to deal with. "They've got thousands of tons of the stuff this close, just sitting, waiting to be hauled away, and they're paying through the nose to get it, and to get it shipped half way across the country."

With great haste George contacted the mining company, made arrangements for removal, and solidified his position with his first two clients with whom he had had only "toehold stature."

Months later he gleefully wrote that one of his clients had doubled his retainer, the other had raised his expense limit . . . and, after word got around that "good old George really knew what he was doing" in the foundry business, he easily and quickly picked up four more good-paying clients.

FROM CORNER LOTS TO PORTABLE BUILDINGS

Ray B. started advertising corner lots, truck stop restaurants, and gas service stations for sale with us, as a Real Estate Broker in a Pennsylvania hamlet, in 1963. We begrudgingly accepted the ads, which more rightly belonged in his local newspaper—not *BUSINESS OPPORTUNITIES DIGEST* with national and international readership coverage—mainly because he raved about what a "wonderful and needed" publication we had (we're vain enough to be swayed by "bucket-full" flattery at times). He also seemed like a thorough, energetic and hard working man, in addition to the charm and good humor he oozed in his letters, which were written (at that time) on stationery of average quality.

Although he was a crack ad writer, as a real estate man—except for cutting of his lengthy ads we never had to change a word—he always ended his letters to us with something like, "Of course, you are the professional ad writer, so please feel free to change the wording in any way you see fit."

We became fond of this B.S.-filled, but likable, guy.

After placing these very small-time ads for several months, five years passed before we heard from him again. One day in 1968 we received a letter from him, this time from a Kansas City office suite number on a better than average, almost impressive looking letterhead. He enclosed several ads offering to buy apartment complexes with a minimum of 150 units and motels with a minimum of one hundred rooms. His covering letter contained the same blarney to the effect that, naturally, because he was just a small-time real estate man, he had no know-how in the art of writing ads. So, we could change them in any way we wished. As before, the ads were beautifully written—not as much as a comma needing to be changed.

Another three years went by. No word.

Then, in 1971, we heard from him again, via letter, this time from Los Angeles, on an absolutely lush symmetrical cream-on-white, 25%-35% rag-content bond letterhead. He was working as a Real Estate Consultant, selling manufacturing licenses for the manufacture of a complete line of portable buildings—everything from outhouse-sized structures to good-sized warehouses. He told us that his average fee per sale was $9,000, and he had made eight sales the previous year. He told us that things were "looking up," but that he'd like to "better himself," and would we send him a copy of our Integrated Marketing Audit form? With all the style and perfectionism of a top Madison Avenue advertising copywriter he again submitted an exceptionally well-written ad, selling his client's portable buildings.

Ray admitted that his first big break came back in 1963, miraculously from one of his corner lot ads.

(Per his request, we sent him a copy of our Integrated Marketing Audit. After all, we *did* want to see him "better himself.")

THE FINANCIAL CONSULTANT WHO GOT FINANCING, FINANCING... AND MORE FINANCING

In the mid-1960s we sent a complimentary copy of our Integrated Marketing Audit to a *Financial* Consultant who wanted to use it. In *every* case, after getting the questionnaire filled in by the *Marketing* Director, he would take it to the *Treasurer* or *Chief Financial Officer*. The two would then use this marketing profile to its best advantage—always developing a more complete and more formal projection-type program—to acquire additional and adequate financing. A few such embellished "Business Plans" went through Financial Finders and Financial Brokers, albeit most of the financing was placed directly with financial institutions of various kinds. This man found the Integrated Marketing Audit to be an important *plus* in his financial consulting work.

THE AUDIT THAT BACKFIRED

Using a *maximized* version of our Integrated Marketing Audit—a full Integrated *Management* Audit—a Consultant made the humble President of a small, failing manufacturing company feel so inept by the many shortcomings that showed up that he (prematurely, according to the Consultant) went through bankruptcy, abruptly ending a high-pay retainer relationship with the Consultant.

The Consultant, relating the sad tale to us on the phone, talked in a low soulful drone. "Just six months . . . six months . . . that's all I needed," he said in a barely audible monotone. He had several Finders lined up who, he was certain, could have provided just what the company needed for a sales and profit turnaround.

While our specialized *Marketing* Audit was a twenty-five-page form which takes one to two hours to fill out, his *Management* Audit was a one hundred and thirty-five-page "encyclopedia." He told us he spent the *whole day* filling it in with the President. Apparently, the wearying marathon was too much for the President, who was a man with feelings of inadequacy anyway, probably largely due to the fact that his predecessor—his father—was a roaring tiger personality, and evidently a man of superior all-around business talents, who was always able to do well, even through the Great Depression. The Consultant told us later that the President had been seriously considering this drastic legal action previously—the Audit only focused his attention more strongly on the necessity, and speeded up the whole process.

(This is probably a prime example of two important no-no points: 1. Improper "sizing up" of the personality involved. And . . . 2. *Overdoing!* Too overpowering a form—a virtual "bright lights" interrogation. We've always advised the "slow work-up" approach in use of the Audit.)

OLD PRODUCT—NEW MARKET

"I just can't see it. I know it's there. Something big. But I just can't see it."

"It's your dime," we answered, in this phone call from a Detroit Subscriber several years ago. "If you want to read the answers over the phone, maybe we can spot it."

After a solid year of trying to land a good account, as a Consultant, for a firm manufacturing parts and equipment for the OEM farm equipment market, the firm finally acquiesced, and consented to fill in the Marketing Audit form with him . . . on a speculative, contingent-fee basis. If he came up with something solid, as a result, they'd talk retainer with him. In short, he first had to act as a Finder, and find something important. They filled in the questionnaire.

"I've read this damned thing over at least ten times and I just can't put my finger on it," he went on, perplexed. "Jack, I know it's got something to do with the mechanical application of a product, but I guess I'm too dumb about anything in engineering to see it."

Now, as far as anything in the engineering or mechanical areas of business goes, we're in the same boat. We know a car has a transmission, driveshaft, valves and brakes. We know that electric motors have armatures, and we're aware of which end of a screw driver to use. That's about it. But our strong suit has always been visualization of *established* product applications to *different* markets, and we had a hunch this might be the key. We had him read the answers, quickly, from Detroit, with us making notes in Farmington, New Mexico.

The answer was there. The "something big" turned out to be a *mulcher* (this checked out months later, after much correspondence and spec interpretation on the part of the company's

Engineers). But the first clue came in the long phone conversation.

The mulcher was used in heavy grain farming. Protected by good patents, it was found that the mass-consumer market could be tapped with a modification of this product, as a rotary lawn mower attachment for household lawn mowers everywhere . . . and at a price that *substantially* undercut competition. For preservation of yards from winter frosts, and as a fertilizer spreader, it was great. Our Detroit Subscriber negotiated a manufacturing license with another manufacturer.

Success again, and a juicy account for the Finder-turned-Consultant!

THE DAISY CHAIN AGAIN

After filling in his own varied version of the Audit with a mail order house, a Chicago Consultant discovered a large hole in the company's line—some concomitant product needs that were a "natural" to fill out the line and make it more competitive.

Unfortunately, he fell into the hands of a fast-talking Business Promoter who promised he could provide all the needed products, for practically pennies, and find them yesterday. Word was spread far and wide, and a large group of "Daisy Chainers" got into the act, bombarding both the Consultant and the mail order house Executive with their "try this" and "I'll get it for you for X% of the first year's sales" letters, and mimeographed contract forms. Ill will developed between the Consultant and his client, and the account was short-lived.

DUMB LUCK SOMETIMES HAPPENS

Our personal preference is for helping the sincere, hard-working person with a dogmatic, never-let-go tenacity jump his income from, say, only $15,000 to $40,000 a year much more than we would the lazy, do-nothing, "write-a-letter-and-expect-a-pot-of-gold-to-fall-in-my-lap" types increase their yearly income as much as twenty-five cents over their "maybe" earnings of $10,000. However, sad to say, the latter category of effort (or non-effort) seems to predominate in the world.

Joe T. fit this latter category perfectly.

He was a third-rate Accountant, working for a second-rate accounting firm in a large Eastern city. He came aboard in 1969 as a *B.O.D.* Subscriber and stayed for six months—six months of pure hell as far as we were concerned. With his first check for a three-month trial subscription came a letter, typed poorly on plain typing paper, and embracing a few misspelled words. He informed us that he was going into the consulting field, "on the side," because his $8,900 yearly salary was inadequate, and that he fully expected, through his subscription, to at least double that income over the next six months, or he would ask for his $6.75 back.

Joe turned out to be a obnoxious "Pen Pal," if there ever was one. We can't remember a week, during that period, when we didn't receive at least one letter from him (always on plain paper with misspelled words). One missive would be a diatribe on all we were doing wrong in the publishing business. The next would be a complaint that he was not getting any answers to his letters of inquiry. The next would be a dissertation on how a management consulting business should be run. All letters to us were interspersed with requests for special, tailor-made, detailed information, research, and time-consuming look-ups.

After he renewed his subscription for a second three-month period, we finally had to tell him, one day, in a long letter, that we were in the publishing business, not the research business . . . that we merely brought key, who-to-contact information together and presented it to him each month through *BUSINESS OPPORTUNITIES DIGEST* . . . and that what he *made* of this information, or *did not make* of it, was entirely up to him.

Then we got a phone call from him. When we refused to accept the collect charges, he decided to pay for the call himself, and came on in a whining, complaining, griping voice. He wasn't getting anywhere in his new consulting business, and, naturally, it was all our fault.

The conversation went something like this:

We asked, "Did you ever have an attractive letterhead made up?"

"No."

"What do you say in your letters?"

"I ask for more information."

"Do you ever follow-up?"

"No."

"Have you studied up, thoroughly, on all aspects of the various consulting fields?"

"I don't have to. I'm an accountant."

Then he went on the offensive with a long series of innuendos and accusations that we weren't doing enough for him.

Totally exasperated at this point, we told him a refund check for the unexpired portion of his second subscription would be in the next mail, and ended with a terse, non-public-relations-like, "good bye!"

The very next day brought a long letter from a man who lived *in the same city as Joe*. He had seen an issue of *B.O.D.* and "let us in" on everything he found wrong with it (for our confidential benefit, of course). He then went on to itemize a long list of requests for all kinds of research information. (Mind you, he hadn't spent a cent; we were expected to *donate* our services.) We were advised of his social and business prominence, his immense stature in his community, his urgent need for the information and his demand for an early response.

"Ye Gods!," we thought, "another Joe!" Although this man was wealthy, the "Odd Couple" fit was simply too fascinating a possibility to be denied.

In our short reply (purposely delayed a few weeks because we fumed over the audacity and presumptuousness of this pompous man) we told him, sorry, but we could not fulfill his many requests, but there was a "Management Consultant" in his city who could most likely be of help. We gave him Joe's name and address.

Some six to eight months later we got a letter from Joe, still on typing paper with the expected misspelled words, saying he'd *finally* landed his first client.

Guess who!

Though he didn't renew his subscription (for this we were grateful), he didn't ask for his money back either.

He even said, "thanks."

GETTING TO THE DECISION MAKER IS OF VITAL IMPORTANCE

Using our Integrated Marketing Audit as his chief tool, Consultant/Finder, Tom O., fell on his face some fifteen times before he "scored."

"They always shuffle me off to the Assistant Advertising Manager, the Market Research Manager's secretary, or some clerk who sits behind a file," he lamented in a phone call to us. "How—for God's sake *how*—do you get to see the Big Wheel?"

Tom was a brilliant young man, an MBA from an Ivy League

School, possessor of a well-organized business mind, and one who didn't know the meaning of the word, "defeat."

Now he was wavering.

Never having met Tom, personally, we couldn't be certain, but, from the way he talked we presumed that his only personality shortcoming was aggressiveness (lack of it).

"It doesn't work all the time," we answered, "but we could suggest something that works often enough so the law of averages should pay off for you."

"What's that?" He was quite anxious to discover some magical secret. To use the word, "curiosity," in describing his reaction would be a gross understatement.

"Nothing mystical," we said, "just walk in like you own the place. After all, if you're well dressed (we just guessed that he was the immaculately dressed, well manicured, type from little clues picked up in a number of prior phone conversations), the poor little receptionist doesn't know whether you're one of ten kids of an itinerant farm worker or a relative of the Rockefeller family."

We went on to say that, with enough forceful air to back him up, he'd be surprised how often he'd be rushed right on through to Mr. Big, the man he'd *have to see* before he could get anything accomplished.

It is a fundamental axiom of American industry, it seems, that Mr. Big *must* be protected, *at all costs,* from the intrusions on his time of Mr. Little. Barbed wire, sand bags, tank traps and land mines are placed in his path. The shuffling of Mr. Little off on the fifth Assistant to the Vice President in charge of Retrogressive Planning is a common ploy. There is only one way to beat the odds: Yes, just like in the movies, *charge through to Mr. Big like a raging bull.* If you're forthright and firm, when trying to line up the appointment with junior Executives (if you glance at your watch a lot, implying that your time is valuable, too, this helps), and take a polite but resolute "let's cut through it" attitude, you'd be surprised how often you'll get through to the real decision maker. Don't forget, while the corporate flunkies and yes men are paid to protect Mr. Big, they can't take the chance of appearing incompetent in his eyes either—unable to recognize a potentially good business deal.

Of course, the phone appointment is *the best* first approach. But, even walking in as a total stranger, we'd say some 15%-20% of the time (a good average) you'll make it on through—in companies employing a hundred or more people. Naturally, the bigger the company, the lower your get-through success-ratio. With the phone as your initial probe, your success-ratio should start out at a much higher rate.

Without *all* the evidences and personal demeanor of culture, refinement—*yet total determination*—we'd guess your chances of "getting through" in *any* company employing a hundred or more people—are but a fraction of 1%.

Tom O. geared himself for the "big push." This must have involved a lot of inspirational-type study and self-push; we didn't hear from him again for nearly two years.

"It took a while, but I finally made it," he wrote. He then related the success he'd had with a particularly choice account—in addition to two small ones—that he'd landed by bulldozing past the usual cordon of "armed guards" and using combined Consultant/Finder techniques to make good money for his new clients . . . and, more importantly, for himself.

FROM FINANCIAL CONSULTANT TO INVENTORY-LIQUIDATOR FINDER

Spotting a repetitious occurrence, one that showed up over and over, and was reflected in the balance sheets of several of the small manufacturing companies he was working for, caused a New York Financial Consultant *to switch fields completely.*

While so many in the financial community put much credence in the *current* ratio portion of a company's balance sheet, which *includes* inventories, the Consultant started *subtracting* this item of "current assets" and made some startling discoveries. Instead of the beautiful and sound-working-capital-position inference of the many three to one and four to one ratios that many Accountants and Investors would interpret, he was finding numerous cases of weak, putrid one to one and one and two tenths to one ratios.

Now, inventories are customarily reported in a lump . . . *but three separate and distinct classifications are covered:* finished products, work-in-process, and raw materials.

Upon delving into the big inventory problems—as shown by the *net quick assets* ratios of such top-heavy-inventory plagued companies, he discovered a bundle of opportunities wherein he could earn considerably more money as a Finder. He found that those companies having an inordinately heavy inventory of finished products were in some kind of sale/marketing "bind." He then proceeded to find surplus products outlets for many lines that were not moving, picking up a fee for each consummated deal, of course. There were little sale possibilities for the work-in-process, so he largely skipped this classification except for a few scrap metal deals. Where he made his biggest fees were in dumpings of the raw materials. For raw materials of just about all kinds—the sometimes wild fluctuations in market prices notwithstanding—there is always a ready and waiting market, somewhere—*if* you know where to look. He *knew* where to look.

A "MINT" TO BE MADE FOR THE MERGER/ACQUISITION SPECIALIST

Of all the fields of Finding, undoubtedly the toughest, most intricate, complex and clandestine—*yet one affording the biggest rewards*—is mergers and acquisitions.

A New Yorker, a man who started out in the securities business, graduated to a high-level position with a holding company, then, as so many millions of men have done over the centuries, got sickened by corporate politicking, in-fighting, inner-sanctum intrigues, and cut out, going "on his own."

As a Consultant/Finder he first brought two small electronics firms together. Then, using the "assets parlay" method, he enabled his combined company/client to buy a bigger firm: a scientific instrument company. With the three in tow he was able to talk a fourth young company into an especially sweet stock swap, because number four was yearning to become a conglomerate (this was in the conglomerate-craze years, 1966-1969), and because the particular tooling and facilities "spread" of his client company was right in the path of the young conglomerate's intended growth.

From this experience he developed a formula:

1. Merge two small technical products companies in *any* field, from the standpoint of marketing facilities compatibility and augmentation. However, the accent had to be on technical superiority, primarily.

2. Parlay the total assets into a larger company bleeding for better technical know-how and distribution facilities. The emphasis here had to be on the outstanding *financial* resources of the third company.

3. With careful steerage, *planned from the beginning,* throw the combination into the path of the dinosaur, the company

devouring everything in its ever-forward-moving footsteps, driven by the hell-bent drive to conglomerate.

We never knew the man, personally, but a Subscriber was, in turn, a friend. According to the resultant hand-me-down information we were able to attain, the Consultant/Finder was instrumental *in closing twelve such mergers in three years.* Purportedly he never earned less than $75,000 on any one deal, and one fee was rumored to have been over $1,500,000.

You figure it.

Money in this field?

Whew!

CHAPTER 9

Pure Finder Case Histories

Now for a variety of unusual and illuminating case histories, involving Finders only—from the files of *BUSINESS OPPORTUNITIES DIGEST* . . .

A YARD FULL OF SHRIMP

Ralph P. was lured by the big money to be made in commodities. Having owned his own fishing boat—but, sadly, knowing little about the *business* end of commodities—he decided to become primarily a land-lubber and set up shop as a Finder. Due to his experience in the fishing business he specialized in sea foods.

(This is one of the zaniest stories we've ever uncovered in our many years in businesses of all kinds.)

In negotiating a big-tonnage shrimp purchase for a client—on a contingent, Finder's fee basis—he overlooked the small detail of the proper delivery instructions. Upon returning from a business trip to his suburban San Francisco home, he approached a porch, garage and back yard piled eye-level high with the pink little appetizers . . . and was confronted by a furious wife.

PRODUCTION FACILITIES OFFERED —VIA COMPUTER

A Midwest service company, maintaining computer data on what kind of production facilities were available throughout the country, closed a lot of deals through Finders. It was a sweet offer: The Searcher paid nothing for use of the service—the companies who paid the fees for having their facilities listed *also* paid the Finders' fees.

SPITE SELDOM PAYS OFF

Stupid is the name of a half Chow and half Malemute dog. (The name was bestowed probably inappropriately.) As a Western Miner's tale of Stupid's lunchtime activities goes: Everyday at high noon an automatic alarm would buzz in the dog's head and he'd trot over to the tunnel just as the workers were sitting down to lunch. From one to the next, right on down the line, the four-legged creature would move, sit up pertly, beg for, and procure, a scrap from each. He was always dutifully fed in this manner, by each and every one of the men.

One day a new man ignored Stupid's hung-look request for sustenance. Consequently, when the men left their lockers after meal time, Stupid followed the offender, cocked his leg at the correct angle . . . and urinated on his lunch box.

We've seen many cases of spite in Finders' fee deals too—far too many Finders acting as Stupid did. One such was an Ohio man who'd worked feverishly for six months to close a deal with a big stake—a Finder's fee of some $45,000. Through pure coincidence two principals met on a Mediterranean cruise and made the *very same* business deal that the Ohio man was dickering on with one of them.

In a rage, the Ohio man filed suit. But, because he'd withheld certain vital information in order to protect himself, prior dates, and the direct contact between principals established him as an outider looking in; he lost the suit.

While Stupid may have experienced a euphoric feeling of satisfaction by defiling the Miner's lunch box, we doubt that many Finders feel the same over the ill-advised law suits they pursue . . . and invariably lose.

FEES FOR FINDING CONCRETE FRANCHISEES

In 1970, a large Canadian concrete manufacturer, producing precast concrete steps, stairs and porches for all kinds of housing—apartments, multiple-residences, mobile homes, etc.—offered Finders' fees for finding *franchised manufacturers* all over the U.S.

Response was big, and quite a few Finders made some good money in this field.

ALL THE SCORPIONS YOUR LITTLE HEART COULD DESIRE

A few years ago an Arizona Subscriber offered 3% Finders' fees for finding buyers of scorpions (yes, the deadly little spider) in lots of 1,000 to 10,000. At the time we wrote, "Don't laugh until you've checked a few research labs and discovered the many valuable uses for these—yuuch!—little creatures."

We never did find out whether any money was made by Finders in this market, obviously a restricted one.

THE S.E.C. AND THE EX-PRESIDENT

Maybe it was his location. Who knows? But, in 1972, a Washington, D.C. Subscriber was put out of the Finding business as the result of a visit, one day, by an S.E.C. Attorney. The Attorney informed him that he could not engage in the Finding business, dealing in securities or other types of financing, without the correct licenses.

"They even call a promissory note a 'security'," he complained to us in a letter which he signed, *(company name)* , followed by *(his name)* , followed by the title, *Ex*-President.

"Big Brother is watching us," is, from time to time, the universal catcall of Financing Finders.

To our way of thinking, in our own lay interpretation of the purpose for which the Securities and Exchange Commission was originally set up, was that it was to protect the public *in general.* We cannot begin to figure what business this Government Agency has getting into the vast realm of *private placement* financing. However, this is one of the reasons we strongly emphasized the imporance of licenses, in earlier chapters, in the fields of financing and real estate especially.

We replied to our dejected Washington, D.C. Subscriber (perhaps too dismissingly glibly) that maybe it was a warm day and the Attorney had nothing to do, so he decided to talk a walk . . . and, because he (the Finder) was so conveniently located, the Attorney then decided to drop in on him and hit him over the head with a club. (Many Government Agencies appear to delight in this "fun" pastime, you know.)

Whatever cloud hangs over this field can easily be counteracted by dealing in many other pure buy/sell fields that the S.E.C. cannot, by any logical elasticizing of the imagination, touch. If the day were ever to come (highly doubtful—this Agency is too small, chronically understaffed, and under-budgeted to touch as much as 1% of the many thousands of *private placement* transactions concluded every day) that this Arm of Government *could* effectively control the activities of *every kind* of Finder dealing in financing, then Big Brother is not only "watching" us—he has us by the throat, is strangling us, snuffing out our very business lives.

IN THE FINDING FIELD AGE IS NO BARRIER

One of the most joyous moments we've had in our many years of publishing Finders' fee offerings and information was in reading a letter in 1973 from a ninety-three year old Subscriber, retired from his full-time business for twenty years, who'd earned $9,000 as a Finder in the sale of some closeout consumer merchandise.

He sounded as happy as a kid fresh out of college who'd collected his first pay check with unexpected fringe benefits reflected on the stub.

This is another of the *big advantages* of the Finding field: It's ideal for the retired person who just isn't tired enough to fill out his life mowing the lawn, sitting in a chaise lounge, or watching TV. And, the retired person *can capitalize on the myriad business contacts he's built up over a lifetime.*

Challenge is kept alive, vitality enhanced, the stimulation of anticipation and expectation sustained at a vigorous level.

CONFLICT OF INTEREST—ALWAYS RESIST THE TEMPTATION

Where does "impropriety" end and "fraud" begin? A real fine point of law often intervenes here.

Difficult for us to understand is that there seems—overall—

to be just about as many unethical Finders operating today as there are ethical ones. And, sadly, from *unethical* dealings the slide begins: to impropriety, to outrightly improper dealings, to fraud, to indictments and criminal charges . . . and, infrequently, even to jail terms. Although from our observation point we'd guess that the ratio of *actual jail sentences* to *those who deserve them* runs something like not more than one in one thousand. However, fines and suspended sentences are more common.

Lots of grief for those who choose the Low Road! *Not worth it!*—to our way of thinking! There are simply too many methods and practices to pursue in this field—*strictly above board and honest, all the way*—from which *you* make money, *your principal* makes money (or gets what he wants), the other-end principal is happy, and all are satisfied, wealthier, and home free from any possible further worries or troubles.

Where the borderline of impropriety begins is with *conflict of interest*—collecting a fee from *both* buyer and seller. A California Finder made a regular practice of this, made a lot of money, made a lot of hard feelings when discovered, and finally made a quick exit from the field when the "heat" was turned up too high for his comfort and liking. To our knowledge he was never indicted for anything, but was driven from a career he enjoyed, one in which he prospered, into another career—public relations; he was an ace huckster—that paid him but a pittance by comparison with his earnings as a Finder.

Moral: When you get *deeply* into the Finding business this temptation will, more than you'd expect, flash before you. Unfortunately, greed, too, can make up a form of perverted motivation. *Resist it*—firmly, decisively, unequivocally, with not as much as 1% compromise. Because the Finding business is entirely a *service,* your *reputation,* built over a period of time, *will become your most precious asset.*

SEMI-PRECIOUS STONES FROM THE ORIENT

Cheap stones, but expensive (and inferior) settings in Taiwan, made for a ripe market for a California Finder who tapped a source in that country for a Chicago Wholesale Jeweler, which had the stones set in this country and sold them at a big mark-up. The Finder's primary item from Taiwan was YAGS (man-made diamonds), selling for $8.00 a carat in 1973.

Another good source he tapped in Korea provided almost unlimited quantities of Smoky Topaz at the unbelievably low price of $1.00 a carat.

His profits?

Who knows? . . . but we'd guess plenty.

FEES FOR FINDING CLIENTS FOR A MOBILE HOME PARK MANAGEMENT SERVICES FIRM

In 1970, this was one of the hottest new service fields going— the *managing* of business operations in the burgeoning mobile home park field, enabling lazy owners to sit back and collect their periodic checks with no effort. Several *BUSINESS OPPORTUNITIES DIGEST* Subscribers made good fees, that year, finding clients for a Midwest firm providing these services.

ONE THOUSAND TONS OF SHARK FINS, ANYONE?

"But you've just gotta find it."

After we'd explained for about the third time that we'd had an office fire in 1972 which destroyed our previous Master Copies of *BUSINESS OPPORTUNITIES DIGEST*, and it was therefore impossible to find the source who had offered 1,000 tons of shark fins for sale a year earlier, our crestfallen Subscriber calling from Oregon finally relented in his insistence that we, somehow, magically produce the name and address for him.

"I've got a buyer and could close the deal this afternoon," he said dejectedly.

Even though we've studied all kinds of commodities, their uses and their markets, we must admit to total ignorance on shark fins. Closest we can figure is shark liver oil, because of its enormous vitamin A and D content being of value to the vitamin market and health food trade. The ad on it we'd published a year before was a "first" with us.

Ironically, about three months after the desperate-appeal phone call we received another ad offering shark fins. Because the product was so unusual, the phone call remained vivid in our mind. We alerted our Oregon man to the new availability, and were later informed that he'd closed the deal.

Fee?

On a sale of *shark fins?*

We never found out, but it must have been a good sized one —his letter had that "about to retire" ring to it.

MONEY IN RENTING ASSETS

In 1970, we carried an ad for a financial firm which *rented* assets at a rate of 5% yearly.

Object: To make it possible for businesses of all kinds to show a *stronger* financial statement in order to get financing. Finders' fees were offered, for finding new customers for this unique service.

It was the only time we ran the ad. The Advertiser was literally engulfed in mail, immersed in all the business they could handle.

A few of our Subscribers later told us that they'd made some good money working on this project alone.

FINDERS' FEES FOR FINDING ANYTHING

Another of the most popular ads we ever ran was in 1970: A large International Trader, who claimed a universal market, advertised for large portions of *anything*, as long as it was in *mountainous volume*. ("Wow!," we thought at the time, "how about a million tons of sage brush?") Naturally, he was overwhelmed with response because he offered Finders' fees.

In this particular case very few deals were closed. As several Subscribers complained, the prices offered were always too low. We only heard of one "close" on this one: the stripped contents of a machine tool plant.

FEES FOR FINDING TV-TIME USERS

A multi-millionaire Businessman who seemed to have a finger in just about every kind of business known to humanity once came up with a strange vest-pocket offer. He'd tied up millions of dollars worth of TV-time for spot commercials. For some reason known only to himself, he refused to deal through the conventional network/syndicator/film production company/advertising agency channels. He advertised for Finders to peddle it for him. From what we could piece together, even though it took a while, the Finders he engaged got rid of it for him.

A DIFFERENT SLANT ON MERGER/ACQUISITIONS

When two companies are merged *all printing has to be changed.* A Southwestern Subscriber specialized in this business and used Finders to bring such potentialities to his attention.

A MATTER OF INTERPRETATION AND LEVEL OF SATISFACTION

What is a fortune?

A "fortune" is a relative thing.

To the hash-house restaurant Dish Washer earning $4,000 a year, $10,000 a year would constitute riches.

To the $7,000 a year Shipping Clerk, perhaps a fortune would be $15,000 yearly.

To the department store Salesman earning $10,000 yearly, we're sure $20,000 a year would be considered wealth.

To the Truck Driver making an annual income of $13,000, $30,000 would seem like a pot of gold.

Even the $50,000 a year Executive, knotted into a huge mortgage on his $60,000 home and college expenses for three children simultaneously, would think that a sudden jump in his income, to $125,000, would constitute a "fortune."

Several years ago, a hard-working young man, a bank Accountant whose annual income could not have pierced the five-figure bracket, took up the ideal part-time activity of Finding. His hobby was coins, so he decided this would be the best and most logical starting point. He not only bought all the books and subscribed to all the magazines on the subject that he could find —periodicals reporting on the field from the *commercial* side—

but made up lists from directories and from the yellow pages of all the near-big-city phone books within easy travel "reach." He gradually built a Finding business of buy/sell contacts. He used his knowledge of markets to collect small fees on a variety of regular transactions.

"I've been averaging maybe $500.00 a month—not a lot of money—but it's fun," he told us in a letter.

We figured the extra $6,000 a year he was pocketing represented, probably, a 50%-75% increase in income over his annual bank compensation. And, starting from such a low "base" this was not appreciable. But the tone of his letter indicated he felt he was now "well-off."

Was he making a "fortune?"

As we said, the whole subject seems to be one of interpretation and level of satisfaction.

HOW ABOUT INDIAN HANDICRAFTS?

Saul G., a New Yorker, was perhaps the least likely of all candidates to take up residence on the Ute Indian Reservation in Southern Utah, after spending a long tenure in his career in the garment business. Saul was thoroughly fed up with the under-the-table dealings, price and throat cutting practices common in this business, rampant on the $24.00 Island.

But Saul's knowledge of the garment business enabled him to quickly see the quality and fad-style-difference possibilities in American Indian-made garments. He quickly re-established contact with many of his old friends and business associates in New York, and acted as a Finder in garment sales to them.

He then moved south and found an even greater variety on the Navajo Reservation in Arizona. He also became interested in Indian handicrafts of all kinds, and found these to be the *best* profit-makers (in terms of sales to that big chunk of our population which resides to the east of the Mississippi), and cashed in.

Still not content, he moved further south, across the border into Mexico. Now his knowledge, and access to the vital product-market link, was like discovering the Lost Dutchman's Gold Mine.

While we never had any direct contact with Saul on anything other than routine matters, word came back to us from several different sources that "Old Saul really had it made."

OFFSHORE FINANCING FOR A HUGE RESIDENTIAL BUILDER

We never learned what this fee added up to, but it must have been monumental. One man collected a 15% fee for his Finder's role in raising offshore financing for the construction of *500,000* homes in South America.

The total fee must have been staggering—perhaps even the all-time record dollar amount.

TWENTY PERCENT INVESTMENTS—GUARANTEED AND SECURED

Another of our Advertisers who was swamped with response was an eastern firm which offered a 20% annual return, guaranteed and secured, on real estate "package" deals. All transactions were attorney-to-attorney, and bank-to-bank.

Because Finders' fees were offered, much activity in this offering went on for an extended period of time. A few Finders had a "field day" working on this one.

UNPATENTABLE IDEAS

Believe it or not there is a market—*much bigger* than you'd think—for *un*patentable ideas.

And, a Texas Subscriber has made quite a business of selling these over a long period of time—through Finders.

HOW ABOUT A TAX-DEDUCTIBLE TRIP TO THE BAHAMAS?

We don't know how this Illinois man managed it. But for years he dealt in real estate, oil and gas, and ranch management operations, offering Finders' fees in cash, *plus* tax-deductible trips to the Bahamas.

WORLD-WIDE COMMODITIES SALES THROUGH A CANADIAN BROKER

A Toronto Finder, specializing in commodities of just about every sort, did such a tremendous business—much of it on a Co-Finder basis with U.S. men—that one of our Subscribers once told us, "Why should I mess around with complicated records and tons of correspondence? I can make a living off this guy alone."

(The Canadian Finder died of a coronary in 1973. We've often wondered how many U.S. Finders died along with him—in the wallet.)

STRAIGHT THROUGH TO WALL STREET

A New York Subscriber who specialized in mergers, acquisitions, and the obtaining of venture capital made good money by paying 6% Finders' fees for the finding of people in the market he was trying to reach: the zillions of Businessmen all over the world in dire need of just such a "short cut" connection.

Connected this man was. In correspondence we never ceased to be in awe of his *pin-point* knowledge. He was *always* "on target." He knew *exactly* where—on "The Street"—to take just about any kind of business "package," project, new venture plan or proposal.

Now retired, he found he couldn't *un*-advertise; too many others continued doing it for him. Word-of-mouth advertising persisted for years. His feats became near-legend, made to seem even greater than they were in all the recountings and stories. He was constantly hounded to come out of retirement.

To escape what he deemed unjust, continuous intrusions on his privacy, he finally fled to Australia to pursue the only thing he wanted left out of life: peaceful, set-your-own-pace retirement (the man was in his late seventies).

SMALL TOOLS, HOUSE AND YARD GADGETS—WHICH WAY TO SWING?

In 1969, a frustrated Inventor, after struggling for more than ten years to get manufacturing and distribution facilities lined up for some fifty patented products he held in the small household tools and gadgets field, without success, turned to Finders.

Yes, it happened!

In 1970, a Finder swung a deal for him that absorbed about 90% of his line.

In 1973, another Finder took care of the other 10%.

By this time he had another ten patents filed, and, last we heard, was still absorbed in various new drafting-board-to-prototype projects—with the intention of continuing to work exclusively through Finders.

TAX HAVEN CORPORATIONS AND FINDERS' FEES TOO

The service of a German Subscriber was to set up tax haven corporations in such remote countries as Andorra, The Bahamas, The Cayman Islands, Campione, Liechtenstein, Luxembourg, Hong Kong, Liberia, Panama, The New Hebrides, Sealand, The Norfolk Islands, and other "New What?" spots.

His fees were ridiculously low (must have done a giant volume of business). Before the stiff U.S. Treasury Department restraints of 1970, more than a few of our Finder/Subscribers made more than a few bucks in fees working with this man.

Since?

Well, we don't know. We haven't heard much on this particular "scene" for some time.

BIG RETURNS ON INDUSTRIAL EQUIPMENT LEASEBACKS

A California Subscriber worked out an intricate arrangement with several Leasors of industrial equipment wherein he could offer returns up to 18% per year on invested capital, *plus* 2% Finders' fees for finding Investors. His methods involved a lot of financial juggling, but apparently he tried with the utmost care to stay completely honest and "above board."

"I've got a Patent Attorney, a former S.E.C. Attorney, a good C.P.A. firm, and a retired Postal Inspector for constant advice on how to stay clean with everybody," he told us in a phone conversation in 1968 or 1969. "So far, no sparks."

He also admitted that he'd done some good business with Finders.

We lost track of this man a year later, and, when we were contemplating investing some money of our own with him, his address turned up as one of the casualties of our 1972 office fire.

(Perhaps we'll get lucky: He'll read this book, and get in touch with us.)

AN ANNUITY-TYPE FEE

One of the more unusual offers we carried was a *$60,000 per year, for twenty years,* fee—for finding $57,000,000 worth of financing for a sour gas recovery plant and system.

It is the rule, rather than the exception, that such huge deals stay open for many months, even years, before they are closed—if ever. As in the case of the man who offered a $4,000,000 Finder's fee on the completed sale of a 3,000,000-acre Canadian Ranch—we've often been curious about the outcome of this one.

A NEW TWIST—"LIMITED PARTNERSHIPS" IN COMMODITIES TRADING

In 1972, a midwestern firm offered "Limited Partnerships" in an off-beat sort of commodities-type syndicate.

From what we were able to gather, it operated, loosely, along the lines of a mutual fund, and the initial claim was one of a guaranteed 11% annual return, fully tax sheltered, somehow.

Two Finders found some "Limited Partners" and picked up some good fees in the doing. But we never learned of this program's growing to any significant degree.

FEES FOR FINDING BASEMENT WATERPROOFING CONTRACTORS

The process for external basement waterproofing was unique and, in 1967, a Finder, well connected with builders and construction people across the country, made a lot of money in fees, lining up contractors everywhere, for the manufacturer, to do the jobs.

In 1969, he expanded his operations into Canada and made a lot of money there, too.

INSTANT PLUMBING

This system, said to save builders and plumbing contractors 10%, *and installable in fifteen minutes,* had a lot of appeal.

Ten percent Finders' fees, for finding builder/contractor/user relationships were offered.

With plumbing costs, especially, among *all* construction costs, going "into orbit," we considered this to be an exceptional opportunity for Finders.

FEES FROM A SWISS BUSINESSMAN

In 1973, a Swiss Businessman (listed in *WHO'S WHO INTERNATIONAL, EUROPE, SWITZERLAND,* etc.) with connections all over Europe and the U.S.—he "commuted" to the U.S. regularly—offered a "generous" Finder's fee for finding a Non-Executive Director seat on the Board of Directors of an American corporation for him.

He had access to much *inside information* on world currency valuations and fluctuations, low taxation incorporation possibilities in Europe, and was able to provide sound counsel on international political and economic affairs. And, in the age of the dollar being kicked around like a football all over Europe, heralding the (???) coming monetary apocalypse, this should be a tempting offering for some U.S. corporation doing much business there, we thought.

We further thought this to be a Finder's fee opportunity *extraordinaire.*

THE MISCELLANEOUS AND THE ODD-BALL

It seems to be as far back as we can remember, but in our blunt fashion, for many years now, we've run some zany Finders' fee offers in the columns of *BUSINESS OPPORTUNITIES DIGEST* . . . a good many with uncerimonious brevity, a few with a bit of cynicism, some with blunderbuss, and others with built-in innuendo-warnings that "this might not be all that it appears."

Examples:

We've published fee offers for finding clients who would *rent* entire marketing organizations . . . for finding buyers of Racing Greyhounds . . . for finding buyers of all kinds of military equipment, including armed jet aircraft . . . for finding sellers of block-mortgage "packages" on ghetto and slum properties . . . for finding Investors for guaranteed endowments (supposedly registered with the Government) . . . for finding Inventors (yes, Inventors, a group probably as large in number as Women's

Libbers) . . . for finding users of shopping center *duck race* traffic building stunts . . . for finding overstocks of *marbles* . . . for finding blacksmith's tools, *worthless* real estate, 1890s-type country store cracker barrels.

We've run ads offering fees for finding buyers of Phoenician burial urns, Ming vases, gold bullion in Mexico, King Solomon's mine . . . for finding sellers of corporate shells of just about every kind, Eskimo-made crafts, divining rods, pre-1880 mining leases.

We've seen just about everything offered in this field—at one time or another—that the human mind could possibly conjure up.

CHAPTER 10

Quickie Review

IN THIS BOOK we have tried covering the entire Finders' fee field, to the best of our ability. As broad, diverse, horizonless as it is, however, we could—really—no more than scratch the surface . . . a twenty-volume set of 1,000-page books each would most likely not even cover 50%. The field, its potential, and its rewards, *are that vast.*

But, we *did* slightly brush, we think, the main and fundamental points. In thinking back over what you have just read, and reading back over the same terrain, these most significant points were:

1. An explanation of what Finders' fees are.
2. How do you start in this business?
3. We tried to emphasize the importance of controlling all initial information, so as to protect yourself and your possible fee.
4. Business correspondence, which has been very successful for us in the field of finding, is a point we perhaps even went overboard on—simply because we feel the area of "impression" is crucial to your success.
5. In brief descriptions we only brushed the most lucrative fields for big earnings and profits. Once again, to get your focus in the right direction, these fields are: commodities, minerals, precious and semi-precious stones, surplus and close-out merchandise (of all types), new products and inventions, exports and imports, collectors' items and antiques, real estate, financing, mergers and acquisitions.

6. *Know your markets,* a cardinal rule of study, preparatory to any proposals, was emphasized.

7. We discussed the pros and cons, advantages and disadvantages, of "going it alone" and business relationship "tie-ins" with so many other types of Businessmen.

8. *Psychology,* as heavily accented in the examples of a variety of letters, was the next step we thought important to work in, as well as "starting point" personal contacts.

9. We endeavored to stress how maximum use of *leverage,* when joined with the proper psychology, can open doors for you that ignoring this tool would keep closed. Many people think of "leverage" as employed in business as a form of arm twisting. This need not be so. It can be used honestly, in a way that is strictly "above-board," and to full effect, to enable you to live with your own conscience.

10. The matter of protecting yourself, through exchanges of letters, agreements and contracts is another subject we tried to hit—though briefly—with a hammer. There's no reason why you can't play the game fairly, *but still protect yourself, legally, to the utmost.*

11. We touched upon bank confirmations, and good banking relationships.

12. We then got into the needed supplies, equipment, organization, and systematizing you'll require once you move into the more "advanced" stages of finding.

13. Pitfalls and Pratfalls. What To Do. What to Avoid. Under this chapter heading we tried to stress two profound and implicit points: Both the necessity of a tie-in, into some kind of Finder network, but, at the same time the avoidance of the "daisy chain" entrapment that so often occurs on *specific* transactions.

14. We touched upon the subject of when to threaten legal action—when not to. And, we emphasized the leverage-power of multiple governmental investigative agency action when you feel that you've been treated unfairly, or outrightly cheated.

15. Within the limitations of space in a small book, we could only glaze the sides of the *raw power* of the Integrated

Marketing Audit, by using only one example—the many ways such a tool can be used in the *manufacturing field.*

In all, we fervently hope this book will give you a start, first, in the proper *thinking* direction . . . then in the proper *action* direction.

A FINAL WORD—ON ATTITUDE BUILD-UP

There is always an enormous market for clubs, organizations, courses, and books of the "pull-yourself-up-by-your-bootstraps" school. Apparently many, many, many people—probably far more than behavioral scientists of all ilks realize exist—*need* words of encouragement, ego build-up, and writings of all kinds in the *inspirational* area. This *must* be the case, else why the overwhelming market, choke-full of such aids and help.

To illustrate the point we're trying to make, a point which ties in, intertwiningly, with the maturing process, let's say that a *total stranger* stops you on the street, and says, "You've got a hard, cold look about you; I'll bet you don't have a friend in the world." What would your reaction, to such a totally unexpected, shocking statement, from a complete stranger, be?

During our lifetime, our reaction would have been something like the following:

Twenty years ago we would have been completely enraged, argued to the point of severe altercation, and tried to "put-the-man-down" as low as we could.

Fifteen years ago we would have just gotten mad, brushed past the man and forgotten about it.

Ten years ago we would have been slightly irritated, thought to ourselves, "this guy's nuts," walked around him, and forgotten it.

Five years ago we would have maybe even smiled a little, but would have wondered about the incident for a while later. Improvement? Yeah! Maybe!

Today we'd probably laugh, making like this was some kind of joke, and say, very politely, "pardon me," and walk off. But, we'd think about it—*not* negatively, but *positively*—in such a way as, "Gosh, that was strange! Why did he approach me and say that? . . . *but* maybe there *was* a germ of something worthwhile in what he said . . . maybe there *are* some ways in which I can *substantially* improve myself, and I should try and figure out how."

The foregoing had only to do with how we, with *our own particular* personality, would have reacted, at various levels of maturity.

Now, let's consider the well-known fact that all people are entirely different—complete and separate entities unto themselves. At any given time, how would *others* react?

One would clobber the guy in the jaw.

One would start a yelling match.

One would want to know the "why" of such a statement, and, defensively, try to argue the answer out of him.

One would be taken completely aback, leave quickly, but associate that spot on the street with the incident every time he walked past it again for many years.

One would leave hurriedly, but wonder, wonder, and wonder, for a long period of time . . . and worry, worry, worry about it.

One would be reminded of the incident every time he heard a similar phrase on television, or read something in the same vein in his business correspondence, books, magazines or newspapers.

Many—maybe even a majority of all people—*would be crushed.* Some would even go right home and cry.

At this point you've got to be wondering, "What has all this got to do with a book on Finders' fees?" The answer is ironic: Before you can hold out any hope in the *Finding* business, you must first "find" yourself.

If you approach the finding business—or *any* business, for that matter—from a negative, "I'm unproven, untried, not as good as other people" view of yourself, you are *incapable* of applying the proper psychological techniques absolutely essential to success.

If this—a basically negative, pessimistic outlook on life—can possibly stand in your way, for "starters" read Og Mandino's, *THE GREATEST SALESMAN IN THE WORLD* (Fell), perhaps the greatest book in the world to start you out of your lethargy, lack of self-confidence, or any other form of negativism. Then follow-up: read *all* of the top best-sellers in this field. Your local book store and library are full of them. And, when you've *changed yourself* (hopefully over a *much shorter* period of time than we've been able to change ourself) you're ready for . . .

THE PATTON TOUCH

The flamboyant and unpredictable World War II General, George S. Patton, was an enigma. He was incorrigibly outspoken, a paradoxical cross-breed of religious and reincarnation beliefs and vile profanity . . . but was, perhaps, *one of the greatest leaders of men in all recorded history.*

Because business in some ways resembles wars—tactics, strategy, maneuvering, logistics, planning and psychology—we thought it fitting to end this book with a few excerpts from the opening speech from the movie, "Patton," delivered by actor George C. Scott, in one of the truly magnificent portrayals of all time. This film clip is now being used widely in U. S. Army training camps as part of its indoctrination courses. In these following excerpts, we tried through punctuation, italics emphasis, and pace, to maintain the *impact* of what Patton thought, devoutly believed, and lived. To quote:

"Men . . . all this stuff you've heard about America not wanting to fight, wanting to stay out of the war, is a lot of horse dung. Americans, traditionally, love to fight. All *real* Americans love the sting of battle . . . When you were kids, you all admired the champion marble shooter, the fastest runner, the big league ball player, the toughest boxer . . . Americans *love* a winner . . . Americans play to win *all the time.*"

The next passage, we feel contains the essence of Patton's *super*-positive attitude, the attitude he propounded and himself practiced in his every action, while drawing every breath, throughout his lifetime:

"Now . . . there's another thing I want you to remember: I don't want to get any messages that we're 'holding our positions.' We're not holding anything. We'll let the Hun do that. We are *advancing constantly* . . . and we're not interested in holding on to anything except the enemy. We're going to hold him by the nose and kick him in the ass . . . *We're going to kick the hell out of him all the time . . .*"

By no exercise of imagination-elasticity can you consider your fellow Businessmen "the enemy." This is not the point. We do not wish to draw any parallels here. Rather, we feel that the *deep significance* of the last quoted paragraph, *as pertains to business,* was the Patton philosophy of *advance, advance, advance* . . . never let up on any of your advantages, your gains . . . strike at opportunity, seize it, ring it for all it's worth, make it work *for* you . . . build on it, parlay it into more and more and more opportunities . . . make them grow, ten, a hundred, even a thousand-fold. *And, grow in stature, self-satisfaction, and enjoyment of life, right along with them.*

It is on this note that we conclude this book.

Appendix—The Finder's Library

THIS SECTION identifies many books, booklets, directories, pamphlets, lists and periodicals of all kinds helpful to the Finder.

Advice: Don't try to purchase *all* of them. If you were to, you'd not only set yourself back over $1,000, but you'd also set yourself back a year or more in the reading time this would necessitate, *before* you could get started in the Finder business.

Instead, cull, select, carefully hand-pick those publications that you think would be tailor-made for *you*. This will not cost you much (many are free or very low-cost) in dollars, and, naturally, the saving in time is pro-rata.

Obviously, we cannot guarantee the perpetual existence of these publications. Publications, like every other kind of products and services in American industry come and go; constantly a "turnover cadence" moves, side-by-side, with time. Therefore, with the presentation of annotations of these publications we cannot endorse, recommend or guarantee accuracy or withdrawals from the market. Most of all, *we cannot guarantee price*.

We have omitted the price from many of these publications for two simple reasons:

1. They have fluctuated so rapidly, naturally in an upward direction, as inflation ever-soars, that we just can't keep up with them. Or . . .
2. We just don't know the price.

Where prices are listed we're a bit more certain of the availability, and, at the price given . . . but, here, too, *we cannot be certain.*

Where prices are listed, you can buy directly from this compilation; where they are not, we'd suggest that you first write a letter of inquiry and obtain the price.

Ruefully, many of your letters will come back marked by the Post Office, "Moved—forwarding time expired." (This is due to a new appendage to the Post Office's credo of higher postage costs, less service.) In 1971, they cut the mail forwarding time from two years to one, so that you, the taxpayer, will be further hamstrung, have a more difficult time getting through to whomever you wish to contact. Of course, where you've sent checks, you'll automatically get the check back in such cases, and where you've merely sent letters of inquiry you simply won't get any answers.

Cheer up, though! Where you send money, *most often* the publisher or distributor will deliver the ordered product. We don't know of too many who will ignore cash orders.

So . . . here you are. For what it's worth, here's an extensive compilation of *the best and most useful literature* you can possibly obtain—in our opinion—to help you get going in the Finders' field.

ACQUISITION & MERGER NEGOTIATING STRATEGY. Book. A score of men responsible for over 1,000 acquisitions and mergers put into print their composite views in this book: the pitfalls; how to determine overall corporate strategy; who should handle negotiations and why; how to determine value and weight risks; how to bring up the subject of price, etc. Price: $25.00 per copy. Distributed by: *B. Klein Publications, Inc., 11 Third St., Rye, New York 10580*

ADVERTISING AGE. Weekly magazine. Covers the advertising industry very efficiently. Published by: *Advertising Publications, 740 Rush St., Chicago, Ill. 60611*

ADVERTISING AND SALES PROMOTION BUYERS GUIDE. Directory. Lists all firms identified with services rendered to the advertising and sales promotion industry. Also includes product listings. Published by: *Advertising Publications, Inc., 740 Rush St., Chicago, Ill. 60611*

AMERICAN ART MUSEUMS. Directory. A listing of American art museums and data on each. Published by: *McGraw-Hill Book Co., 330 W. 42nd St., New York, New York 10036*

AMERICAN DROP-SHIPPERS DIRECTORY. Booklet/Directory. Lists and describes some 500 sources which will drop-ship their products, and another 200 which will sell wholesale in small lots. Price: $2.75 per copy. Distributed by: *Business Opportunities Digest, 301 North Orchard Ave., Farmington, New Mexico 87401*

AMERICAN REGISTER OF EXPORTERS AND IMPORTERS. Directory. Lists over 25,000 U.S. Exporters and Importers classified by products. Also lists banks in world trade, American chamber of commerce agencies in foreign countries, buying agencies, custom house brokers, and other valuable lists concerned with foreign trade. Distributed by: *B. Klein Publications, Inc., 11 Third St., Rye, New York 10580*

AMERICAN SCIENCE MANPOWER. Directory. Some 300,000 scientists are listed in the National Register of Scientific and Technical Personnel lists compiled and published by the U.S. Government. Price: $2.00. Published by: *Superintendent of Documents, U.S. Government Printing Office, Washington, D.C. 20402*

AMERICAN SOCIETY OF ARMS COLLECTORS. Directory. Listings of 170 members of the American Society of Arms Collectors. Gives names, addresses and specialties in arms collecting. Published by: *Samuel E. Smith, Box 313, Markesan, Wisconsin*

AUDARENA STADIUM GUIDE. Directory. A listing of 2,300 auditoriums, exhibit halls, arenas and stadiums. Managers' names and addresses are included. Price: $20.00. Published by: *Amusement Business, Billboard Publications, 1719 West End Ave., Nashville, Tenn. 37203*

AUSTRALIAN OPPORTUNITIES HANDBOOK. Booklet. Comprehensive guide gives latest information on employment, land, free agricultural assistance, and many other subjects. Price: $1.00 per copy. Published by: *International Publications, P.O. Box 29193, Indianapolis, Ind. 46229*

BACON'S PUBLICITY CHECKER. Directory. Rundown of information of all kinds on approximately 4,000 magazines and daily newspapers. Published by: *Bacon's, 14 E. Jackson Blvd., Chicago, Illinois 60604*

BANKS AS A CAPITAL SOURCE. Booklet. Tells how banks look at loans; what you must offer; how they will judge you as a prospective borrower; the banker's secret checklist for approving loans so you can best determine how to prepare your application; how to pyramid bank credit enabling you to get loans from several banks at the same time; how to set up a multi-bank line of credit using the bank's own money; much more. Price: $2.00 per copy. Published by: *Second Income News, Box 2506, Santa Rosa, Calif. 95405*

BARGAIN BUYERS GUIDE. Booklet. Lists more than 100 unique and unusual bargain/opportunities, including where to get some publications of good "inside-information" help. Price: $2.00. Published by: *World Wide Trade Service, P.O. Box 283, Medina, Washington 98039*

BREAK EVEN POINT STUDIES FOR SMALL MARKETERS. Pamphlet. Price: Free. Published by: *Small Business Administration, Washington, D.C. 20416*

BUILDING STRONG RELATIONS WITH YOUR BANK (Small Marketers Aid #107). Pamphlet. Price: Free. Published by: *Small Business Administration, Washington, D.C. 20416*

BUSINESS & CAPITAL REPORTER. Monthly newsletter. Lists and describes about 40-75 business opportunities in each issue, in detail. Many of the offerings have Finders' fees attached. Price: $100.00 per year. Published by: *National Counselor Reports, Kerryville, Texas*

BUSINESS BUYER'S GUIDE. Booklet. 200 things you should know before buying a business! Which businesses are the best prospects for a buyer; how to buy a business that is not for sale; how to deal with business brokers, and how not to; which brokers can help you, which can't; the truth about "asking prices;" how to learn the real truth about how much a business has been earning for its present owners; a quick course in how to analyze financial statements; many other "inside-information" points are covered. Price: $3.00 per copy. Published by: *Second Income News, Box 2506, Santa Rosa, Calif. 95405*

BUSINESS CAPITAL SOURCES. Book/Directory. A long introduction, covering the subject of long-term and short-term capital needs, precedes a Directory listing several thousand capital sources. Price $15.00. Published by: *International Wealth Success, P.O. Box 186, Merrick, New York 11566*

BUSINESS FORECASTING METHODS. Book. Gives basis for making short-term, cyclical, and long-range forecasts by measured and methodical steps. Describes methods of forecasting industry, company trends. Published by: *Holt, Rinehart and Winston, Inc., 383 Madison Ave., New York, New York 10017*

BUSINESS OPPORTUNITIES DIGEST. Monthly newsletter. Written and edited by the author of this book. Each issue contains 150-400 business opportunity listings and news items of all kinds, including approximately 25-75 *specific* Finders' fee offers. Some 20% of the content is "open" (full contact names and addresses published) and 80% are coded listings (blind box type). Price: $24.00 per year; $6.75 for 3-month trial subscription; $1.00 for a sample copy. Published by: *Business Opportunities Digest, 301 North Orchard Ave., Farmington, New Mexico 87401*

BUSINESS PUBLICATION RATES AND DATA. Monthly Directory. Contains full advertising and circulation rate data on some 3,000 business publications categorized into 175 markets. Also lists 200 international publications used by U.S. advertisers. Published by: *Standard Rate & Data Service, Inc., 5201 Old Orchard Rd., Skokie, Illinois 60076*

BUSINESS WEEK. Weekly Magazine. Good general business and economics magazine. Published by: *McGraw-Hill Publishing Co., Inc., 330 West 42nd St., New York, New York 10036*

CAPITALIST REPORTER. Bi-monthly Magazine. Includes interesting business aricles, some with contact information. A large classified section adds to this publication's appeal as a contact-reference source. Price: $9.00 for 12 issues. Published by: *The Capitalist Reporter, 150 Fifth Ave., New York, New York 10011*

CASH VALUES IN INDUSTRIAL SCRAP (Technical Aid

#45). Pamphlet. Price: Free. Published by: *Small Business Administration, Washington, D.C. 20416*

CERAMIC DATA BOOK BUYERS DIRECTORY. Directory. Gives information on 3,000 ceramic equipment and raw materials manufacturers and suppliers in this field. Published by: *Cahners Books, 89 Franklin St., Boston, Mass. 02110*

CHEM SOURCES. Directory. Listings cover 600 organic and inorganic chemical producers and suppliers. Covers 36,000 chemicals. Price: $30.00. Published by: *Directories Publishing Co., Flemington, New Jersey 08822*

CITY DIRECTORY CATALOG. Directory. A listing of every city directory in North America. Published by: *Association of North American Directory Publishers, 270 Orange St., New Haven, Connecticut 06509*

CONSULTANTS AND CONSULTING ORGANIZATIONS. Directory. Covers some 3,000 consultants and firms. Gives fields of specialties. Published by: *Publications Section, Graduate School of Business and Public Administration, Cornell University, Ithaca, New York 14850*

CRAFT, MODEL AND HOBBY INDUSTRY. Directory. Lists 1,000 manufacturers and wholesalers of craft, model and hobby merchandise. Published by: *Hobby Publications, Inc., 229 W. 28th St., New York, New York 10001*

DESIGN OF RESEARCH INVESTIGATIONS. Booklet. Gives the approaches to marketing problems through research. Covers such subjects as setting up research design, development of plans, types of analysis, and pretesting. Published by: *American*

Marketing Association, 230 North Michigan Ave., Chicago, Illinois 60601

DEVELOPING A LIST OF PROSPECTS (Management Aid #188). Pamphlet. Price: Free. Published by: *Small Business Administration, Washington, D.C. 20416*

DIRECTORY OF AMERICAN IMPORTERS AND EXPORTERS. Book/Directory. Extensive guide and listing. Price: $5.00 per copy. Published by: *World Wide Trade Service, P.O. Box 283, Medina, Washington 98039*

DIRECTORY OF ARTS & CRAFTS MATERIALS. Directory. 3,000 manufacturers and distributors of art, craft, ceramic, and related supplies are given. Published by: *Art Material Trade News, 1517 W. Fullerton Ave., Chicago, Illinois 60614*

DIRECTORY OF CONSULTANT MEMBERS—AMERICAN MANAGEMENT ASSOCIATION. Directory. Gives an alphabetical, classified listing of approximately 700 consulting firms and individual consultants who are members of the American Management Association. Included are brief descriptions of each Member/Consultant's field of specialty. Published by: *The American Management Association, 135 W. 50th St., New York, New York 10020*

DIRECTORY OF NATIONAL ASSOCIATIONS OF BUSINESSMEN. Booklet/Directory. Price: 50¢. Published by: *Superintendent of Documents, U.S. Government Printing Office, Washington, D.C. 20402*

DIRECTORY OF NATIONAL TRADE AND PROFESSIONAL ASSOCIATIONS OF THE U.S. Directory. An alphabetical listing of over 4,000 U.S. professional and trade associations. Published by: *Columbia Books, Inc., 917 15th St. NW, Washington, D.C. 20005*

DIRECTORY OF UNITED STATES IMPORTERS. Directory. Complete data on 30,000 U.S. and Canadian Importers—company name, address, phone number, types of merchandise imported, bank references, custom house brokers, etc. Price: $60.00. Published by: *The Journal of Commerce, 445 Marshall St., Phillipsburg, New Jersey 08865*

DIRECT SELLING ASSOCIATION MEMBERSHIP DIRECTORY. Booklet/Directory. Lists 160 members. Published by: *Direct Selling Association, 1730 M St. NW, Washington, D.C. 20036*

DISCOVER AND USE YOUR PUBLIC LIBRARY (Management Aid #202). Pamphlet. Price: Free. Published by: *Small Business Administration, Washington, D.C. 20416*

DISTRIBUTION SOURCES—THE MANUFACTURERS AND INVENTORS SOURCE-LIST OF MARKETING CHANNELS. Pamphlet. Lists 70 sources—all the way from those offering worldwide distribution down to those covering large (several states) territories. Included are a few who will finance. Price: $1.00 per copy. Published by: *Business Opportunities Digest, 301 North Orchard Ave., Farmington, New Mexico 87401*

DON'T BANK ON IT. Book. Gives in vivid detail the inside workings of banks; shows how Investors can make up to 13% on their money, all fully insured. Replete with a large number of little-known facts about our country's banking system. Good knowledge for the Financial Finder, particularly, and all Finders in general. Price: $8.98 per copy. Published by: *Jay Norris Corp., 6338 Lindmar Dr., Goleta, Calif. 93017*

ELEMENTS OF MARKETING. Book. A comprehensive text concerning marketing functions, policies, prices, transportation, processes, and channels. Deals with both consumer and industrial aspects, including statistics and recent developments. Gives many reference listings and appendices on marketing costs and retail trade movements. Pubilshed by: *Prentice-Hall, Inc., Englewood Cliffs, New Jersey 07632*

ENCYCLOPEDIA OF LITTLE-KNOWN, HIGHLY PROFITABLE BUSINESS OPPORTUNITIES. Book. By the author of this book. Covers the how and where of just about every form of business and investment opportunity known. Finders' fees; unusual franchise/distributorship/agents wanted; import/export; part-time ventures; unique speculative, special situation, mineral, commodities, and real estate opportunities; mergers/acquisitions; sources of financing, manufacturing, and sales help. Reveals how many business promoters become wealthy through such methods as parlay, pyramiding, using trusts, checkerboarding, bank-to-bank deals, leverage, and working on other people's money. Price: $9.95 per copy. Published by: *Frederick Fell, Publishers, Inc., 386 Park Ave. S., New York, New York 10016*

EXHIBITS SCHEDULE. Directory. Alpha-listing of convention and trade show exhibit opportunities for your services or products. Covers around 5,000 trade shows, expositions, and fairs. Price: $35.00. Published by: *Sales Meetings, Directory Dept., 144 E. 44th St., New York, New York 10017*

EXPANSION AND CAPACITY DIGEST. Directory. More than 200 publications are abstracted—those useful in locating articles for use in market research, economic forecasting, sales prospecting, and financial analyses. Price: $100.00. Published by: *Predicasts, Inc., 10550 Park Lane, Cleveland, Ohio 44106*

FELL'S COMPLETE GUIDE TO BURIED TREASURE, LAND AND SEA. Book. Lists hundreds of sunken treasure ships by location and abandoned mines in the U.S. For the derring-do Finder this book can be a useful source-tool to establishing rapport with highly-speculative-minded principals. Price: $5.95 per copy. Published by: *Frederick Fell Publishers, Inc., 386 Park Ave. S., New York, New York 10016*

FELL'S UNITED STATES COIN BOOK. Priceless to the Finder active in the coin field. Has latest and complete data on buying, selling, evaluating, with complete data on every coin ever minted by the United States Government. Price: $3.95 per copy. Published by: *Frederick Fell Publishers, Inc., 386 Park Ave. S., New York, New York 10016*

FINANCING SOURCES. Lists over 300 money sources. All kinds: private, public, "risk" funds, loan correspondents, financial institutions, venture capital organizations, others. Also describes the kinds of financing specialized in by each. Some will pay Finders' fees. These are also designated. Price: $2.75 per copy. Published by: *Business Opportunities Digest, 301 North Orchard Ave., Farmington, New Mexico 87401*

FINDERS FEE GUIDE. Booklet/Directory. Describes over 140 *specific* Finders' fee opportunities, with full names and contact addresses given. Covers further instructions on how to negotiate a Finder's fee agreement. Price: $2.75 per copy. Published by: *Business Opportunities Digest, 301 North Orchard Ave., Farmington, New Mexico 87401*

FIREARMS ENCYCLOPEDIA. Directory. Lists manufacturers, suppliers, associations, publications, dealers, gunsmiths, and importers. Published by: *Shelley Braverman, Athens, New York 12015*

FOREIGN GOVERNMENT PURCHASING AGENCIES IN THE UNITED STATES. 4-page folder. Lists 100 sources—only those agencies having specific buying authority—embassies and legations which act only in a liaison capacity have been omitted. Price: $1.00. Distributed by: *Business Opportunities Digest, 301 North Orchard Ave., Farmington, New Mexico 87401*

FOREIGN TRADE CLUBS IN THE UNITED STATES. Booklet/Directory. Lists clubs in the U.S. interested in importing, exporting, and foreign trade. Price: Free. Published by: *United States Chamber of Commerce, 1615 H St. NW, Washington, D.C. 20006*

FOREIGN WHOLESALE DIRECTORY. Booklet. Tells where to obtain products of all kinds, from all over the world, at below-wholesale prices, get samples for yourself, lists suppliers and drop-shippers, and sources of free foreign wholesale catalogs and trade directories. Price: $1.00 per copy. Published by: *International Publications, P.O. Box 29193, Indianapolis, Ind. 46229*

FUNDAMENTAL RECORDS FOR SMALL MARKETERS. Pamphlet. Price: Free. Published by: *Small Business Administration, Washington, D.C. 20416*

GEBBIE PRESS ALL-IN-ONE DIRECTORY. Directory. Contains information on over 20,000 publicity outlets in the U.S. Radio, TV, newspapers, magazines, farm publications, news syndicates. Presents names of editors, frequency of publication, circulation data, and descriptions of facilities, other information about most major media. Price $40.00. Published by: *Gebbie Press, Box 1,000 New Paltz, New York 12561*

THE GREATEST SALESMAN IN THE WORLD. Book. Motivational. The best starting point for would-be Finders with self-starting problems. Price: $4.95 per copy. Published by: *Frederick Fell Publishers, Inc., 386 Park Ave. S., New York, New York 10016*

THE GREATEST SECRET IN THE WORLD. Book. By the author of *THE GREATEST SALESMAN IN THE WORLD*. Further motivational theme. Ideal starting-point, not only for Finders, but for Businessmen in any line of endeavor who, at times, find themselves holding themselves back, through procrastination, inertia, or indecisiveness of any kind. Price: $4.95 per copy. Published by: *Frederick Fell Publishers, Inc., 386 Park Ave. S., New York, New York, 10016*

GUIDES FOR PROFIT PLANNING. Booklet. Price: 25¢. Published by: *Superintendent of Documents, U.S. Government Printing Office, Washington, D.C. 20402*

GUIDE TO AMERICAN DIRECTORIES. Directory. Carries complete information on over 4,500 directories of every kind, covering more than 300 trade, educational, and professional categories. Data include name of publisher, price (many are free). Fully indexed. Price: $30.00 per copy. Published by: *B. Klein Publications, Inc., 11 Third St., Rye, New York 10580*

GUIDE TO BUSINESS & INVESTMENT SERVICES. Booklet/Directory. Categorizes over 600 different business and investment services. Price: Free. Published by: *Select Information Exchange, 2095 Broadway, New York, New York 10023*

GUIDE TO EXCEPTIONAL MONEY-MAKING OPPORTUNITIES. Booklet/Directory. Reports hundreds of prime Finder's fee, franchise, sales, investment, and "special situation" opportunities of every kind. Price: $2.75 per copy. Published by:

Business Opportunities Digest, 301 North Orchard Ave., Farmington, New Mexico 87401

GUIDE TO PUBLIC WAREHOUSES. Directory. A compilation of names and addresses of public warehouses in the U.S. and Canada. Listed alphabetically, by city and state. Published by: *Distribution Worldwide, Chestnut & 56th Sts., Philadelphia, Pa. 19139*

GUIDE TO SELF-INCORPORATION. Book. Step-by-step instructions; complete state-by-state cost schedule for starting a $100,000 corporation; complete kit of necessary forms—charter, by-laws, banking resolutions, first meeting, first directors' meeting, etc.—and reveals many little-known corporate structure advantages. A "Do-It-Yourself Incorporation Guide." Price: $4.95 per copy. Published by: *Second Income News, Box 2506, Santa Rosa, Calif. 95405*

GUIDE TO VENTURE CAPITAL FINANCING. Booklet. Published by: *American Science Associates, 1345 Ave. of the Americas, New York, New York*

HANDBOOK FOR SMALL BUSINESS. Book. Gives information on Federal programs helpful to small business. The programs range from business development and financial assistance to technical information, patents, and research. Price: $1.75. Published by: *Superintendent of Documents, U.S. Government Printing Office, Washington, D.C. 20402*

HOW TO ANALYZE YOUR OWN BUSINESS (Management Aid #46). Pamphlet. Price: Free. Published by: *Small Business Administration, Washington, D.C. 20416*

HOW TO BECOME A MANUFACTURERS REPRESENTATIVE. Booklet. Gives the how and where. Much source information, for further study, is included. Price: $2.00 per copy. Published by: *Second Income News, Box 2506, Santa Rosa, Calif. 95405*

HOW TO BUY A SMALL BUSINESS. Booklet. A short guide. Includes tables, charts, and checklists. Price: $1.00. Published by: *Pilot Books, 347 Fifth Ave., New York, New York 10016*

HOW TO EARN TOP DOLLARS IN DIRECT SELLING. Book. The psychological aspects of direct selling and the Finding business are so similar as to be twin-like, in many respects. You should find this book a fine "preparatory tool." Price: $5.95 per copy. Published by: *Frederick Fell Publishers, Inc., 386 Park Ave. S., New York, New York 10016*

HOW TO FINANCE A GROWING BUSINESS. Book. Undoubtedly the best *all-around* book on the "how-to" of financing ever written. Every detail of this complex field is spelled out and pin-pointed. It's a veritable "college course" in business finance. Price: $9.95. Published by: *Frederick Fell Publishers, Inc., 386 Park Ave. S., New York, New York 10016*

HOW TO GET $50,000 WORTH OF SERVICES FREE, EACH YEAR, FROM THE UNITED STATES GOVERNMENT. Book. Choice information for the Finder. Tells the where and how of all facets (an unbelievably large amount) of help, aids, and precious business research information—all free, or next-to-free—from the U.S. Government. Price $7.95 per copy. Published by: *Frederick Fell Publishers, Inc., 386 Park Ave. S., New York, New York 10016*

HOW TO GET PEOPLE TO THINK AND ACT FAVORABLY WITH YOU. Book. Psychology is so vitally important to the Finder that this fine book should be of infinite help in getting established. Price: $5.95 per copy. Published by: *Frederick Fell Publishers, Inc., 386 Park Ave. S., New York, New York 10016*

HOW TO INVEST. Booklet. Published by: *Standard & Poor's Corp., 345 Hudson St., New York, New York 10014*

HOW TO MAKE A LIVING OR A SMALL FORTUNE WITH A TELEPHONE. Booklet. While the first of two sections will not be of much interest to Finders ("How To Set Up And Operate A Telephone Answering Service"), the second section should be of value. It shows how big merchandise deals are being made every day, all over the country. Gives specifics, techniques, all the how-to data. Price $3.00 per copy. Published by: *Second Income News, Box 2506, Santa Rosa, Calif. 95405*

HOW TO PROFIT FROM THE COMING LAND BOOM IN THE CARIBBEAN ISLANDS AND LATIN AMERICA. Book. Includes detailed sections on: Location and size, weather, characteristics of the people, race relations, structure of Governments, the political picture, state of the economy, internal and external transportation, existing tourist facilities, tax structures, incentives and laws affecting the investment of outside capital, current prices, and risks involved. Price: $9.95. Published by: *Frederick Fell Publishers, Inc., 386 Park Ave. S., New York, New York 10016*

HOW TO READ FASTER AND REMEMBER MORE. Book. Learn how to double, triple, or even quadruple your reading speed while you develop an astonishingly effective and masterful memory at the same time. A different approach to speed reading. Helpful to hyperactive Finders. Price: $8.95 per copy. Published by: *Frederick Fell Publishers, Inc., 386 Park Ave. S., New York, New York 10016*

HOW TO SELL YOUR IDEAS. Book. Exhaustive and penetrating study of the development and protection of ideas. Price: $5.95 per copy. Distributed by: *Second Income News, Box 2506, Santa Rosa, Calif. 95405*

HOW TO START YOUR OWN BUSINESS. Booklet. Blankets most major aspects: what business should you choose; how to get the money; where to locate; how to buy a going business; managing it; record keeping; laws and regulations; taxes; more. Price: $3.00 per copy. Published by: *International Publications, P.O. Box 29193, Indianapolis, Ind. 46229*

HOW TO SUCCESSFULLY INVEST IN REAL ESTATE. Booklet. Published by: *Horizon Corp., 4400 E. Broadway Blvd., P.O. Box 5626, Tucson, Ariz. 85703*

HOW TO TURN YOUR IDEAS INTO DOLLARS. Booklet. Provides a step-by-step formula for the bringing into being of profitable ideas, then going on to market them. Price: $2.00. Published by: *Pilot Books, 347 Fifth Ave., New York, New York 10016*

HOW TO USE THE CHESKIN SYSTEM FOR BUSINESS SUCCESS. Book. A thorough treatment and instruction "Bible" on avoidance of marking mistakes, and, on the positive side lays out a scientific system for predetermining the effect, or effectiveness, of every facet of marketing—product formulation, styling, brand names, packaging, marketing themes, advertising, much more. Price: $9.95 per copy. *Frederick Fell Publishers, Inc., 386 Park Ave. S., New York, New York 10016*

HOW TO WHOLESALE FOR PROFIT. Booklet. Price: Free. Published by: *Specialty Merchandise Corp., 6061 DeSoto Ave., Woodland Hills, Calif. 91364*

IMPORTERS AND EXPORTERS TRADE PROMOTION GUIDE. Book. Exhaustive and complete guide to doing business overseas. Price: $5.00 per copy. Published by: *World Wide Trade Service, P.O. Box 283, Medina, Washington 98039*

IMPORTERS CONFIDENTIAL DROP-SHIP DIRECTORY. Booklet. Guide to products available for import to the U.S. Price: $2.00 per copy. Published by: *World Wide Trade Service, P.O. Box 283, Medina, Washington 98039*

INDIAN ARTS AND CRAFTS. Two leaflet Directories. Sources of American Indian and Eskimo arts and crafts. Given alphabetically, by state. Each listing tells source, address, city, reservation, products, etc. Price: Free. Published by: *Indian Arts and Crafts Board, U.S. Dept. of Interior, Room 4004, Washington, D.C.*

INDUSTRIAL RESEARCH LABORATORIES OF THE U.S. Directory. Presents full details on thousands of companies maintaining full industrial research laboratories. R & D capabilities are itemized. Price: $42.50 per copy. Published by: *R. R. Bowker Co., 1180 Ave. of the Americas, New York, New York 10036*

INDUSTRIAL WASTE AND SALVAGE. Directory (2 volumes). A listing of waste and salvage facilities of industrial plants and municipalities, including descriptions. Production, utilization, and marketing of scrap, waste, and salvage are included. Price: $15.00 per set. Published by: *Atlas Publishing Co., 130 W. 42nd St., New York, New York 10036*

INFORMATION PLEASE ALMANAC, ATLAS AND YEARBOOK. Book. News events, facts, figures, statistics covering world history and people. Historical facts on sports, education, colleges and universities, and U.S. Government Agencies. Published by:

Dan Golenpaul Associates, 160 Central Park S., New York, New York 10019

INNOVATION: HOW MUCH IS ENOUGH? (Management Aid #173). Pamphlet. Price: Free. Published by: *Small Business Administration, Washington, D.C. 20416*

INTERNATIONAL TRADE FAIRS. Directory. A listing, by country and product, of the many trade fairs held throughout the world. Price: Free. Published by: *Pan American World Airways, Cargo Advertising Dept., 200 Park Ave., New York, New York 10017*

INTERNATIONAL WEALTH SUCCESS. Monthly newsletter. Content is made up of business opportunities of all kinds, with some emphasis on business financing. Approximately 175-250 *specific* contact-sources are presented in each issue, all are of the "open" type—full names and addresses are printed. Many Finders' fee opportunities are included. Price: $24.00 per year. Published by: *International Wealth Success, Box 186, Merrick, New York 11566*

INTRODUCTORY GUIDE TO EXPORTING. Booklet. Published by: *Bureau of International Commerce, U.S. Dept. of Commerce, Washington, D.C.*

INVESTOR'S GUIDE TO STOCK MARKET PROFITS IN SEASONED AND EMERGING INDUSTRIES. Book. The value of this book goes far beyond any applications to the stock market. The analyses of every industry and field and supplemental data are so deep and meaningful that we recommend this as one of the best books ever written—for the extra-sharp, "read-between-the-lines" Finder. Price: $14.95 per copy. Published by: *Frederick Fell Publishers, Inc., 386 Park Ave. S., New York, New York 10016*

KEEP POINTED TOWARD PROFIT (Management Aid #206). Pamphlet. Price: Free. Published by: *Small Business Administration, Washington, D.C. 20416*

LAND OPPORTUNITY REVIEW. Monthly newsletter. Covers land bargain buys in all fifty states: low cost summer homesites, farmland, investment property. Regular monthly features include "Your Fortune In Real Estate," a section devoted to inside tips, and "The International Scene." Price: $10.00 per year; $5.00 for a 4-month trial subscription. Published by: *International Publications, P.O. Box 29193, Indianapolis, Ind. 46229*

LEADING ADVERTISERS IN BUSINESS PUBLICATIONS. Directory. Lists about 2,500 advertisers who have spent $30,000 or more in advertising in business publications. Published by: *The American Business Press, 205 E. 42nd St., New York, New York 10017*

MAIL ORDER BUSINESS DIRECTORY. Directory. Lists more than 5,000 mail order houses. Many are constantly looking for new and different items to include in their catalogs. Price: $25.00 per copy. Published by: *B. Klein Publications, Inc., 11 Third St., Rye, New York 10580*

MAIL ORDER IDEA BOOK. Booklet. Title is a bit of a misnomer. Contains a veritable gold mine of brain-joggers which can be adapted to, and used in, just about every kind of business known, in addition to mail order. Price $1.00 per copy. Published by: *Second Income News, Box 2506, Santa Rosa, Calif.*

MAIL ORDER PRINTING GUIDE. Booklet/Directory. Lists sources of over 100 mail order printers and office supply firms—affording discounts of up to 50% of the prices asked in any given local community. Useful for equipment and supplies sources for

Finders. Price: $2.00. Published by: *World Wide Trade Service, P. O. Box 283, Medina, Washington 98039*

MANAGEMENT AUDIT FOR SMALL RETAILERS. Booklet. Price: 35¢. Published by: *Superintendent of Documents, U.S. Government Printing Office, Washington, D.C. 20402*

MANAGEMENT IN MARKETING. Book. Presents the managerial approach to marketing. Published by: *McGraw-Hill Book Co., 330 W. 42nd St., New York, New York 10036*

MANAGEMENT OF A SALES FORCE. Book. Good step-by-step instruction manual covering this critical area of marketing. Published by: *Richard D. Irwin, 1818 Ridge Rd., Homewood, Illinois 60430*

MANUFACTURERS' AGENTS GUIDE. Directory. A listing of over 11,000 manufacturers who distribute their products through manufacurers' agents and representatives. Published by: *Manufacturers' Agent Publishing Co., 663 Fifth Ave., New York, New York 10022*

MARKET FINDER. Book. 777 aids to marketing new products are given and described in "how-to" detail. Price: $5.00 per copy. Published by: *Second Income News, Box 2506, Santa Rosa, Calif. 95405*

MEMBERSHIP LIST—AMERICAN INSTITUTE OF CERTIFIED PUBLIC ACCOUNTANTS. Directory. Lists 50,000 members of the American Institute of Certified Public Accountants. Published by: *American Institute of Certified Public Accountants, 666 Fifth Ave., New York, New York 10019*

MONEY-MAKING SECRETS OF THE RICH. Booklet. A bunch of wealth secrets, including: how to "wheel and deal" with your banker; how to cash in on the world's biggest lottery; how to open a secret Swiss bank account; how and where to get capital; how to buy U.S. Government land for as little as $3.00 an acre (or even free, in isolated cases); how to get the U.S. Government to finance your business; how to make a fortune in real estate. Price: $2.00 per copy. Published by: *International Publications, P.O. Box 29193, Indianapolis, Ind. 46229*

MONEYTREE. Monthly newsletter. Has a variety of good consumer and business tips, *and sources.* Written in short, tight fashion, each issue contains many up-to-the-minute ideas. Sometimes a column of "wants," mostly in collectors' items and antiques, is run. Price: $10.00 per year; $1.00 for a sample copy. Published by: *Moneytree Club, Kerrville, Texas 78028*

NATIONAL ROSTER OF REALTORS DIRECTORY. Directory. Lists 85,000 members of the National Association of Real Estate Boards. Published by: *Stamats Publishing Co., 427 6th Ave. SE, Cedar Rapids, Iowa 52406*

NEW PRODUCT ANNUAL. Directory. Lists industrial instruments, apparatus, components, materials and equipment which have laboratory application. Includes new literature on certain products, services, and equipment—presented by classification of product category. Published by: *Industrial Research, Beverly Shores, Ind. 46301*

NEW PRODUCT INTRODUCTION FOR SMALL BUSINESS OWNERS. Booklet. Price: 30¢. Published by: *Superintendent of Documents, U.S. Government Printing Office, Washington, D.C. 20402*

ONE HUNDRED AND ONE SHORT CUTS IN MATH ANYONE CAN DO. Book. If you're not a slide-rule Whiz, you'll need all the short-cuts you can get, in applications to business math, in many areas of the Finding field. Price: $3.95 per copy. Published by: *Frederick Fell Publishers, Inc., 386 Park Ave. S., New York, New York 10016*

ONE HUNDRED FIFTY QUESTIONS FOR PROSPECTIVE MANUFACTURERS. Booklet. Excellent checklist. Price: 25¢. Published by: *Superintendent of Documents, U.S. Government Printing Office, Washington, D.C. 20402*

OPPORTUNITIES IN CANADIAN GOVERNMENT LAND. Booklet. Tells where and how to acquire summer cottage sites, recreational lands, farm lands, and wilderness areas, sometimes at give-away prices. Much on lands suitable for investment for less than $1 per acre. Opportunities in every Province are covered. Price: $1.00 per copy. Published by: *International Publications, P.O. Box 29193, Indianapolis, Ind. 46229*

OPPORTUNITY SEARCH. Folder. Good analysis of business conditions, fields, and markets in which to operate. Price: $1.00 per copy. Published by: *Sherwood Publishing Co., P. O. Box 517, Brundidge, Alabama 36010*

OUR NATURAL RESOURCES: HOW TO INVEST IN THEM. Book. Good overall evaluation. Will make you knowledgeable in this field, one of the biggest profit-makers for Finders. Price: $6.95 per copy. Published by *Frederick Fell Publishers, Inc., 386 Park Ave. S., New York, New York 10016*

PREPARING EFFECTIVE PRESENTATIONS. Booklet. A simplified procedure for putting together business presentations that pay off. Price: $2.50 Published by: *Pilot Books, 347 Fifth Ave., New York, New York 10016*

PREPARING FOR NEW MANAGEMENT (Management Aid #183). Pamphlet. Price: Free. Published by: *Small Business Administration, Washington, D. C. 20416*

PRICING ARITHMETIC FOR SMALL BUSINESS MANAGERS. Booklet. Price: 30¢. Published by: *Superintendent of Documents, U.S. Government Printing Office, Washington, D.C. 20402*

PROFITABLE PART TIME, HOME BASED BUSINESSES. Booklet. Price: $2.00. Published by: *Pilot Books, 347 Fifth Ave., New York, New York 10016*

SELECTED LIST OF CONSUMER AND TRADE PUBLICATIONS. Directory. Entries on 4,000 trade and consumer publications, classified by fields of interest. Published by: *Burelle's Press Clipping Bureau, 165 Church St., New York, New York 10007*

SMART-MONEY SHORTCUTS TO BECOMING RICH. Book. Title is self-explanatory. Lays out a compendium of clever, ingenious methods. Published by: *Parker Publishing Co., Inc., West Nyack, New York 10994*

SPECIALTY FRANCHISE / DISTRIBUTORSHIP / AGENTS WANTED REPORT. Contains nothing commonplace; only the unusual, unique, low-cost, and non-competitive type franchise offerings are reported (approximately 110). Price: $1.75 per copy. Published by: *Business Opportunities Digest, 301 North Orchard Ave., Farmington, New Mexico 87401*

RED BOOK. Directory. Alphabetical listing of Hong Kong manufacturers and exporters with addresses, telephone numbers, products, type of business, etc. For years Finders have had much success dealing with this, the "Shopping Center" of the Western World. Price: $15.00. Published by: *World Wide Trade Service, P.O. Box 283, Medina, Washington 98039*

REDUCING THE RISKS IN PRODUCT DEVELOPMENT (Management Aid #82). Pamphlet. Price: Free. Published by: *Small Business Administration, Washington, D.C. 20416*

RESEARCH CENTERS DIRECTORY. Directory. A listing of 6,500 university-related and independent (non-profit) research organizations. Depicts the activities and fields of interest of each. Price: $47.50. Published by: *Gale Research Co., Book Tower, Detroit, Mich. 48226*

SALES AND MARKETING EXECUTIVES INTERNATIONAL—ANNUAL REPORT AND DIRECTORY. Directory. Lists 500 officers and directors of affiliated clubs of the Sales and Marketing Executives International. Published by: *Sales and Marketing Executives International, 630 Third Ave., New York, New York 10017*

SALESMAN'S OPPORTUNITY MAGAZINE DIRECTORY ISSUE. Listings of specialty sales firms and their products. Published by: *Salesman's Opportunity Magazine, 1460 Hancock Center, Chicago, Illinois 60611*

SALES POTENTIAL AND MARKET SHARES (Small Marketers Aid #112). Pamphlet. Price: Free. Published by: *Small Business Administration, Washington, D.C. 20416*

SECOND INCOME NEWS. Newsletter. Includes applicable business information of every kind, including some data and contact information for Finders. Strong in how-to articles, and new and original ideas. Price: $1.00 for a sample copy. Published by: *Second Income News, Box 2506, Santa Rosa, Calif. 95405*

SHOESTRING MARKETING GUIDE. Booklet. A complete "short course" in how to take a product to market . . . and, how to do it cheaply. Includes sections on free sources of information, packaging, pricing, market research, selling consumers, retail and wholesale outlets, engaging agents and brokers. Price: $2.00 per copy. Distributed by: *Business Opportunities Digest, 301 North Orchard Ave., Farmington, New Mexico 87401*

SMALL BUSINESS PROFITS FROM UNPATENTABLE IDEAS (Management Aid #53). Pamphlet. Price: Free. Published by: *Small Business Administration, Washington, D.C. 20416*

STATISTICS SOURCES. Directory. An elaborate coverage of 16,000 sources of reliable statistical information on approximately 11,000 subjects. Arranged in dictionary form. Price: $27.50 per copy. Published by: *Gale Research Co., Book Tower, Detroit, Mich. 48226*

SUCCESS UNLIMITED. Monthly Magazine. Covers the inspirational, motivational, and how-to fields very well. Includes regular monthly columns by W. Clement Stone and Paul Harvey. Price: $5.85 per year; sample copy 60¢. Published by: *Success Unlimited Magazine, The Arcade Building, 6355 Broadway, Chicago, Illinois 60626*

SURPLUS DEALERS DIRECTORY. Directory. Listings of about 3,000 Surplus Dealers. Published by: *Institute of Surplus Dealers, 303 W. 42nd St., New York, New York 10036*

SURPLUS RECORD. Monthly magazine. Contains names and addresses of many industrial machinery and equipment dealers and names and addresses of those dealers in rebuilt and used industrial machinery. Published by: *Thomas P. Scanlan, 20 N. Wacker Dr., Chicago, Ill. 60606*

TRADEMARK REGISTER OF THE UNITED STATES. Lists 350,000 trademarks currently registered in the United States Patent Office, from 1881 to date. Alphabetical, by class, with date of registration. Price: $29.50. Published by: *Trademark Register, 422 Washington Bldg., Washington, D.C. 20005*

TRUTH IN LENDING. Pamphlet. Explains the fine points of the Truth in Lending law. Price: Free. Published by: *Consumer Product Information, Washington, D.C. 20407*

UNDERSTANDING THE COMMODITIES FUTURES MARKETS. Booklet. Price: 50¢. Published by: *New York Mercantile Exchange, 6 Harrison St., New York, New York 10013*

UNITED STATES GOVERNMENT PURCHASING, SPECIFICATIONS, AND SALES DIRECTORY. Booklet/Directory. Price: 60¢ Published by: *Superintendent of Documents, U.S. Government Printing Office, Washington, D.C. 20402*

U.S. GOVERNMENT SURPLUS DIRECTORY. Shows how to buy such products as jeeps (low as $62, as is), autos, boats, airplanes, guns, and thousands of other items. Tells how, who, what, where! A Bidder's Mailing List Application Form is included. Price: $1.50 per copy. Distributed by: *Business Opportunities Digest, 301 North Orchard Ave., Farmington, New Mexico 87401*

UNUSUAL INVESTMENT OPPORTUNITIES. Booklet. All

outside-the-stock market, it covers such areas as ranch and cattle management, oil, gas, mining, leasebacks, mortgages, and other kinds of out-of-the-ordinary opportunities. Price: $1.50 per copy. Published by: *Business Opportunities Digest, 301 North Orchard Ave., Farmington, New Mexico 87401*

UP YOUR OWN ORGANIZATION. Book/Directory. Brilliantly organized, well-written, this book "covers the waterfront" of entrepreneurship. Such subjects as new product and marketing planning, personal preparation, the business plan, data on invention and idea conceivability, sources of financing, plant location, marketing strategy and motivation, and availability of management assistance of all kinds are only a few examples of what this giant book engenders. Price: $14.95. Published by: *Entrepreneur Press, Mission Station, Drawer 27591, Santa Clara, Calif. 95051*

VERIFIED DIRECTORY OF MANUFACTURERS' REPRESENTATIVES. Directory. Geographic listing of 15,000 manufacturers in the U.S. and Canada, dealing in all products (other than food). Price: $30.00. Published by: *Manufacturers Agent Publishing Co., 663 Fifth Ave., New York, New York 10022*

WASTE TRADE DIRECTORY OF THE WORLD. Directory. Lists, geographically, 70,000 dealers, brokers, packers, importers, and exporters, and graders of scrap and waste materials. Also, contains lists of consumers of scrap steel from mills, foundries, paper and woolen mills, shredders, manufacturers and distributors of equipment and supplies. Price: $25.00. Published by: *Atlas Publishing Co., 130 W. 42nd St., New York, New York 10036*

WHAT IS THE BEST SELLING PRICE? (Management Aid #193). Pamphlet. Price: Free. Published by: *Small Business Administration, Washington, D.C. 20416*

WHO'S WHO. Directory. Includes biographical material on approximately 40,000 prominent individuals in all fields and in all areas of the globe. Information on outstanding men and women, their educational backgrounds, birthdates, affiliations, addresses, and fields of prominence. Published by: *Macmillan Co., 860 Third Ave., New York, New York 10022*

WHO'S WHO IN ASSOCIATION MANAGEMENT. Directory. 3,500 members of the American Society of Association Executives are listed, each entry showing company and industry. Price: $50.00 (to non-members). Published by: *American Society of Association Executives, 1101 16th St. NW, Washington, D.C. 20036*

WORLD GUIDE TO TECHNICAL INFORMATION AND DOCUMENTATION SERVICES. Lists 273 centers around the world that offer technical information services, including documentation. Published by: *Unesco Publications Center, P. O. Box 433, New York, New York 10016*

WORLD TRADE PUBLICATIONS DIRECTORY. Handy pocket list. Describes 130 publications from 55 countries. (Includes 24 obtainable free.) Price: $1.00 per copy. Distributed by: *Business Opportunities Digest, 301 North Orchard Ave., Farmington, New Mexico 87401*

WORLD WIDE CHAMBER OF COMMERCE DIRECTORY. Directory. Contains alpha-geographical listings of 5,500 chambers of commerce in the United States. Published by: *Johnson Publishing Co., Inc., Box 455, Loveland, Colo. 80537*

WORLDWIDE RICHES OPPORTUNITIES. Directory (2 volumes). Lists 5,000 overseas firms seeking a variety of U.S.

products. Each firm's needs are described in detail giving names, addresses, and complete contact information for each firm. Also includes a list of overseas lenders who finance U.S. exports and imports. Price: $50.00 per set. Distributed by: *B. Klein Publications, Inc., 11 Third St., Rye, New York 10580*